This

... is an authorized facsimile made from the master copy of the original book. Further unauthorized copying is prohibited.

Books on Demand® is a publishing service of UMI®. The program offers digitally scanned, xerographic reprints of more than 152,000 books that are no longer in print.

The primary focus of Books on Demand is academic and professional resource materials originally published by university presses, academic societies, and trade book publishers worldwide.

*The Gospel
in Solentiname*

The Gospel in Solentiname

Volume II

Ernesto Cardenal

Translated by Donald D. Walsh

ORBIS BOOKS
Maryknoll, New York 10545

Third Printing, October 1985

The Catholic Foreign Mission Society of America (Maryknoll) re-
cruits and trains people for overseas missionary service. Through
Orbis Books Maryknoll aims to foster the international dialogue
that is essential to mission. The books published, however, reflect
the opinions of their authors and are not meant to represent the
official position of the society.

Originally published as *El evangelio en Solentiname*, vol. 1, pp.
137–261, copyright © 1975 by Ediciones Sigueme, Salamanca,
Spain

English translation copyright © 1978 by Orbis Books,
Maryknoll, New York 10545

Orbis paperback edition 1982

Library of Congress Cataloging in Publication Data

Cardenal, Ernesto.
    The Gospel in Solentiname.

    Translation of El Evangelio en Solentiname.
    Dialogues on the Gospels between the author and community
members of Solentiname.
    1. Bible.   N.T. Gospels—Criticism, interpretation, etc. I. Title.
BS2555.2.C27713   226'.06   76-2681
ISBN 0-88344-175-6 (v.2)

CONTENTS

v

INTRODUCTION

In Solentiname, a remote archipelago on Lake Nicaragua with a population of *campesinos*,[1] instead of a sermon each Sunday on the Gospel reading, we would have a dialogue. The commentaries of the *campesinos* are usually of greater profundity than that of many theologians, but of a simplicity like that of the Gospel itself. This is not surprising: The *Gospel,* or "Good News" (to the poor), was written for them, and by people like them.

Some friends urged me not to let these commentaries be lost, but to put them together and publish them as a book. That's the reason for this book. I first began collecting them in my mind, insofar as I could. Later, with more common sense, we used a tape recorder.

Many of these commentaries were made in the church, at Sunday Mass. Others were made in a thatched hut opposite the church, used for meetings and the communal lunch after Mass. Occasionally, we would have the Mass and the Gospel dialogue in the open air on other islands, or in a small house that we could get to by rowing along a beautiful river through very tropical vegetation.

Each Sunday we first would distribute copies of the Gospels to those who could read. There were some who couldn't, especially among the elderly and those who lived on islands far away from the school. One of those who could read best (generally a boy or a girl) would read aloud the entire passage on which we were going to comment. Then we discussed it verse by verse.

We used the Protestant translation entitled *Dios llega al hombre,* which is the best translation of the Gospels that I know. The translation is anonymous, but it was unquestionably made by a poet. It is in the simple language of the Latin American *campesino,* but it preserves a maximum fidelity to the Scriptures.[2]

I'm sorry I can't include the many good dialogues we had before we began to collect them—they were carried off by the wind of the lake—nor some others we had when our tape recorder had broken down. But these dialogues have been lost only for this book, not for those who took part in them and who in some way retain them even though they may not remember them.

The archipelago of Solentiname has thirty-eight islands; some are very small, and only the largest are inhabited. The population is about a thousand, composed of some ninety families. The houses are usually thatched huts, all spread out, some distance apart, on the shores of the different islands. On one point of the largest island we established our little community or lay monastery, Our Lady of Solentiname. To this community came the Colombian poet William Agudelo and his wife, Teresita, and their two small children, Irene and Juan; and also some young people born on these islands: Alejandro, Elvis, and Laureano. Communication with the outside was infrequent, and our contemplative retirement was not disturbed in this place, fortunately hard to reach, outside the paths of merchants and tourists.

Not all those who lived on these islands came to Mass, many because they had no boat, and others because they missed the devotion to the saints, to which they were accustomed. Others stayed away through the influence of anti-Communist propaganda, and perhaps also through fear.

Not all those who did come took an equal part in the commentaries. There were some who spoke more often. Marcelino is a mystic. Olivia is more theological. Rebeca, Marcelino's wife, always stresses love. Laureano refers everything to the Revolution. Elvis always thinks of the perfect society of the future. Felipe, another young man, is very conscious of the proletarian struggle. Old Tomás Peña, his father, doesn't know how to read, but he talks with great wisdom. Alejandro, Olivia's son, is a young leader, and his commentaries are usually directed toward everyone, and especially toward other young people. Pancho is a conservative. Julio Mairena is a great defender of equality. His brother Oscar always talks about unity. The authors of this book are these people and all the others who talk frequently and say important things, and those who talk infrequently but also say something important, and with them William and Teresita and other companions that we have had and who have taken part in the dialogues.

I am wrong. The true author is the Spirit that has inspired these commentaries (the Solentiname *campesinos* know very well that it is the Spirit who makes them speak) and that it was the Spirit who inspired the Gospels. The Holy Spirit, who is the spirit of God instilled in the community, and whom Oscar would call

Introduction

the spirit of community unity, and Alejandro the spirit
of service to others, and Elvis the spirit of the society
of the future, and Felipe the spirit of proletarian struggle, and Julio the spirit of equality and the community
of wealth, and Laureano the spirit of the Revolution,
and Rebeca the spirit of Love.

NOTES

1. *Campesino* is literally one who lives in the *campo* (country,
field). Most *campesinos* are farm workers, but some are
fisherfolk.—D.D.W.
2. The Gospel quotations in this edition are my translations from
the Spanish of *Dios llega al hombre.*—D.D.W.

1.

The Ones Sent by John the Baptist

(Matthew 11:1–11)

We read that John, who was in prison, heard about the works of Jesus and sent his disciples to ask him:

Are you the one who is to come or do we wait for another one?

OLIVIA: "I imagine John knew he was going to die. He knew the regime he was living under. And he asked that question so his disciples would know that there was going to be somebody else who would replace him, so they would know that the Messiah was already here. I don't believe he would have doubted. And he asked it so that the disciples wouldn't be discouraged when he died, for he had to die for freedom, and Jesus had to die for the same reason. Their fate wasn't to triumph but to die."

REBECA: "I was thinking the same as Doña Olivia. And I also think John knew that Jesus was the Messiah, but he sent his disciples so

that people would know that it was Jesus and
not him, because a lot of people thought John
was the Messiah."

LAUREANO: "Also so they wouldn't be waiting for somebody else. They'd already made a
mistake the first time when they believed
John was the Christ and he wasn't. Then
somebody else came along, and maybe now
they'd think that later still another one would
come."

I said (and this I had heard from Merton)
that it was also possible that John, in a deep
depression in his prison, might be doubting
that Jesus was the Liberator. John had already announced it in very strong words. He
had said that Jesus was "with his shovel
ready" to separate the wheat from the chaff.
The gospel says that from prison he heard of
Jesus' "works." But maybe those works didn't
convince him. He saw his mission as a failure,
his end very near, and Jesus without any
power. . . . And we read the answer of Jesus:

Tell him how the blind see,
the lame walk, the lepers are clean,
the deaf hear, the dead are resurrected,
and to the poor the good news is announced.

FELIPE: "He doesn't want to talk just with
words but also with deeds. If he said it just
with words maybe they wouldn't have believed him. He says: 'see all the freedom I'm
bringing.' "

ALEJO: "People frightened by the changes

that Christianity is going through should pay attention to this. Jesus doesn't say to them: 'Notice that in such and such a place people are fasting, are praying a lot, are going to Mass every day; he simply sends word to John that people are being cured, getting food, having their problems solved. He's saying that people are being freed.''

I said that Jesus didn't clearly say he was the Messiah, no doubt because it was dangerous to say so. He never said it clearly until they were condemning him to death in the Sanhedrin. What he did here was to say it indirectly to John in such a way that John could understand it: quoting to him the prophecies of Isaiah, that when the Messiah came the blind were going to see, the deaf were going to hear, the lame would leap like deer, the dead would come to life again, the poor would learn the good news of their freedom.

ALEJO'S MOTHER said: "The poor don't have any freedom, not even freedom to think, and then they can't think about the oppressed situation they're in, and they don't even know they're oppressed, and that message is for them. . . . I can't explain it well . . . that message of freedom. . . . The poorest of us feel humiliated, in a situation where we can't even think about freedom or reach it; and if we do manage to think about it, we can't reach it. And that's why Jesus brings us that good news about a change: that all of us poor people in the country are going to have freedom."

And another: "At times you're afraid of the

authorities, you say maybe: 'I'd better not say
anything about this, I'd better keep quiet.' If
you free yourself from that fear and dare to
speak up, and to act, which is more important
than speaking, if you've devoted your life to
God, and if you're ready to sacrifice your life,
then what's going on in us is that freedom that
Jesus is talking about to John the Baptist."

Another said: "And if we repeat that message of freedom, the good news for the poor, we
have to suffer the persecution of the powerful.
They persecute us like Communists. And of
course it has to be that way because they also
persecuted Christ and that's why he died."

PANCHO spoke: "But Jesus was talking
about freedom from sin and not about a physical freedom!"

FELIPE: "Freedom from sin and physical
freedom are the same thing. To keep ourselves
in poverty is a physical slavery, right? And it's
a sin too. Then what's the difference between
physical freedom and freedom from sin? Sin is
physical too. And to save ourselves we also
need physical things."

GLORIA: "And here he says that the good
news is for the poor, that is, for people suffering from an economic, physical slavery."

LAUREANO: "Jesus began to bring about a
physical liberation, for the blind were physically blind, the lame were physically lame.
... And then he says that they hear the good
news of their freedom."

OSCAR: "It says that they were blind, that
they were lame, and that Jesus performed the

miracle. I think it wasn't that Jesus performed the miracle of curing those illnesses but that he freed them from their slavery. They were just the way we are now, just as we're completely blind to reality (which is also physical); as we're deaf to the truth (we just hear the propaganda of the loudspeakers)."

And happy is he who is not scandalized by me.

I said that the exact translation is "he who is not disillusioned about me" and that the word "scandal" comes from the Greek and means "stumble"—literally a stone on which you could stumble in the road.

FELIPE: "It can happen that people are more devoted to money or an easy life, and then they abandon the word of God; those people have become disillusioned with Christ."

REBECA: "To keep believing in him, in spite of all the difficulties, that's what it means not to become disillusioned with him, it seems to me."

OSCAR: "Many could have become disillusioned because he had not come as a powerful king but as a poor man. This could be like a stumbling block for them, in trying to follow him. And I think to give the good news to the poor was a scandal."

Another added: "And John the Baptist, who was in prison, could also get disillusioned about him. Maybe that's why Jesus said what he did."

When they had left,
Jesus began to talk about
*   John to the people, saying:*
"What did you go to see in the desert?
A reed shaken by the wind?
If not, what did you go to see?
A man dressed in luxury?
You know that those who dress in luxury
are in the palaces of the kings."

OLIVIA: "A reed that bends is a weak thing. They didn't go to see a man crumbling before power but a man standing tall. That's why he was in prison. And they didn't go to see a rich man. The rich aren't out in the desert preaching the word of God. They're in the palaces."

Another said: "They went to see a humble man, one who wasn't on the side of oppression but on the side of the people."

And another: "Herod was a very cruel dictator who killed children, and also a millionaire who lived in a palace. Jesus wants to point out the great difference. One was a messenger who was announcing the liberation of the poor. The other wanted all the poor to be his slaves."

In truth I say to you
that of all the people
who have lived up to now,
no one has been greater
than John the Baptist;
nevertheless the smallest one in the kingdom
*   of heaven is greater than he.*

LAUREANO: "Maybe he means that former greatnesses are just shit compared with the kingdom of Christ."

PANCHO: "He says that John was the greatest here on earth but that in heaven anybody is greater."

I said to Pancho that Jesus didn't say "heaven" but "kingdom of heaven," which is the same as the kingdom of God, or God's government in the world. John had preached that that kingdom was "near," and Jesus later announced that it had arrived; so he can't mean heaven.

REBECA: "The kingdom of God is love, that I know. But this confuses me."

I said: "When the disciples were discussing which of them would be the greatest in the kingdom, Jesus put a little boy in their midst. Don't you think that here too he means that in this kingdom the poorest and the most humble are the greatest? The most famous aren't the greatest, even when it's a question of the greatness of a prophet."

OLIVIA: "Maybe it's to give us more encouragement, so that we won't feel weak or unhappy?"

JULIO, Rebeca's son: "Wouldn't it be so that we poor people won't lose heart? So we won't say: We're the last because we're poor and we can't do anything?"

I said: "I've just discovered this during this reflection with you: Jesus is saying that the kingdom of heaven is the kingdom of the poor and humble. John was the greatest prophet, but you, the poor and humble, are even greater. Here there will be no one who rules others, not even as a 'great prophet,' as a 'great leader.' Or you could say that here those who rule are the tiniest ones, the most humble, the poorest."

REBECA: "It's through humility that they rule, and through love. And Saint John was a great man because he was humble, because he wasn't in the palaces of the kings like the rich. That's why he was in prison."

I said: "There is a phrase I often read in Cuba: 'In this revolution the only privileged ones are the children.' And that's true; there the only privileged ones are the children, not the leaders. And it seems to me that Jesus is saying something similar about the kingdom of heaven, that in it the only greatness is in the little ones. And what Laureano said is very true: that all the former greatness is just shit compared with the greatness of this kingdom."

2.

"Come to Me and Rest"

(Matthew 11:25–30)

This time we had Mass on the opposite shore, in a humble village called Papaturro, on the bank of a river in the forest, almost on the border of Costa Rica. A group of us from Solentiname had gone, and in a little church surrounded by cacao trees we discussed these verses with the people from Papaturro:

> *At this time Jesus said:*
> *"I praise you, Father,*
> *Lord of heaven and earth,*
> *because you have revealed to simple people*
> *the things that you hid*
>   *from the clever and the learned.*
> *Yes, Father,*
> *because this is the way you wanted it."*

I asked: "What do you think, Olivia?"

She answered: "It seems to me that Jesus is saying that the wisdom of the world is of no value for God. That is, in the eyes of God. Because it seems to me that it's a wisdom based on money. Somebody who has no money can have just one kind of wisdom: spiritual. Money

9

is the basis of that other wisdom, and so it's a wisdom opposed to equality and love."

I said that Olivia was quite right, that that's an unjust wisdom, because it's a result of economic inequality and at the same time a cause of more economic inequality. In our system education is the monopoly of the rich. For example, here where we are, there are uneducated people only because there are poor people. But God's system is the reverse of ours: God gives his wisdom to simple people and hides it from the clever and the wise. That's why Jesus praises the Father: because that wisdom is an act of justice.

FELIPE: "I see things the way Doña Olivia does. The ones who think they're smart are really from the upper classes, the ones who can study to be engineers, get their high school diploma, or anything. And their wisdom is really for inequality, for their business."

I said that the same thing happened in the time of Jesus. The wise and the clever belonged to the upper class, and those were the ones who rejected him. The ones who followed him were simple people who couldn't read, and those were the ones who understood his message.

FELIPE: "There was that King Herod, who was one of the powerful ones and one of the ones who thought they were wise in those days. He had already decided to kill Jesus. And he brought together all those teachers and clever men so they could tell him where the Messiah would be born. But God hid his knowledge from these people too, and revealed it to the humble people, to the shepherds."

I said Matthew had told us a little earlier that Jesus had sent out his disciples to announce the kingdom. Now it seems that Jesus already found out that his message hadn't been a success among the upper classes. He saw that it was only the simple people who were with him. But he didn't consider this a failure. He didn't feel bad about it. He thanked God that this was the way it was.

LAUREANO: "That's just what's happening now. The poor are the revolutionary class."

ALEJANDRO: "It seems to me that the knowledge a diploma stands for isn't much, because somebody who gets one, the way things are now, doesn't know anything else. For the fellow that's a doctor or an engineer, medicine or engineering absorbs him completely. So he spends his whole life just on that. But the simple fellow is more open to other things, because he really isn't tied to a single thing. Instead he just thinks in his simple way. . . . The lady that's doing the laundry, well, she's thinking about a lot of things while she's doing the wash. And also when you go out to the country—it's simpler and you think more sincerely."

"It's the wisdom that work gives you," I said.

The teacher from a little rural school close by said: "It seems to me that wisdom is love of God. And work is love of God too, isn't it? Because with work we improve things, or we're putting something here that wasn't here before. We're being useful. And that must be why

the worker has a wisdom denied to somebody
who doesn't work but just exploits the work of
others. It seems to me that in this world we all
ought to have a job, and we all ought to have
love for God so that we'll know more."

FELIPE: "And really, true wisdom is what
you learn in order to love others, what you
learn so you can share with others. Ideas and
things you own, too. False wisdom is what you
learn just for your own personal good."

An old man from Papaturro said: "That's
the wisdom of selfishness, isn't it?"

I said that education in our system is the
privilege of a few. To have it is like having
capital, because with it you exploit the labor of
the others who don't have capital. But it's the
uneducated majority who have paid for the
education of those few.

And ELVIS: "But sometimes we who have
the privilege of receiving the other wisdom,
we're selfish too and we don't share it. It seems
to me that we have to share it and we have to
work so everybody can have it."

And another of the young people from Solentiname said: "That's why it's a good thing
that the brothers and sisters from Solentiname have come to share this with the
brothers and sisters in Papaturro."

My Father has given it all to me.
No one really knows the Son
    except the Father;
and no one really knows the Father
    except the Son
and those to whom the Son
    makes him known.

OLIVIA: "I believe that when you love others you love God. Because we don't know God, in the sense that we can't see him. We haven't seen him, neither the Father nor the Son, the way we see our neighbor. We can't say: 'Let's give these five pesos to God,' then. But when we really love our neighbor, we're seeing the Father, and it's because Jesus is making him known to us."

I said: "The fact that the Father has given him everything seems to mean that the Father has transmitted all his knowledge to Jesus. In those days when there weren't any schools that gave diplomas you learned a trade by working as an apprentice with a master. But generally the son learned from his father. Jesus learned carpentry from Joseph. And in the same way, as he tells us here, the revelation that Jesus brings he learned from his Father. This revelation is that God is love and that to love your brother is to know God. In the Bible 'to know' is like 'to love,' and even the sexual act is called 'knowing.' So you can also say, as Olivia did, that anybody who loves his brother loves God. And this knowledge that Jesus brings, and that he learned as a son apprenticed to his Father, is love."

"And he makes it known to the people he loves: to the humble, . . . " said someone from Papaturro.

Come to me,
all you who are weary of your labors
and your burdens,
and I will give you comfort.

FELIPE: "I think he's seeing the suffering of the people more than anything else. We bear the burden of exploited people too. . . . And I think this is the burden Jesus is talking about, and that he wants to ease."

The TEACHER: "Undoubtedly he doesn't call the rich and powerful but the people who have burdens. It's a call to the exploited from everywhere, seeing also that they're weary of their labors. In those days the world was full of slaves, and it's just the same today, except that they're called workers. To all of them he offers comfort."

CARLOS: "This comfort he offers is not for tomorrow but for today. And he gives this comfort through struggle. And it's not that the poor are going to live like the rich but instead with a new sense of life that the people who cling to their wealth can never know."

ALVARO GUZMAN: "He's come to free people with burdens, people overwhelmed by the weight of all the dictatorships of the earth. He's brought love so that he's the one who governs us and so that he organizes all human life, putting an end to exploitation, giving us the comfort of no more injustice."

Accept the yoke that I put upon you,
and learn from me,
for I am patient and humble of heart;
and you will find rest for your souls.

FELIPE: "It seems to me that the yoke he's

talking about is love, the yoke of loving
others."

I said: "Yes. There was a lot of talk in those
days about the 'yoke of the law'; when Jesus is
talking about his yoke he's saying his law: the
law of love."

FELIPE: "And he tells us to learn from him,
that is, to follow his example by fighting for
the liberation of the people. He died because
he was against the rich and on the side of the
humble."

The TEACHER: "And he says that he's patient and humble of heart, not because he was
submissive to oppression but because he was
able to endure in that struggle, and because
his heart was always on the side of the humble
and the poor and not on the side of the proud
and the rich. And he says, 'Learn from me,'
because he wants us to be his disciples in that
struggle and to learn from him to have the
patience to put up with all the sufferings and
humiliations."

Another from Papaturro: "We always live in
a poor and humble way, but we have to struggle as he taught us to achieve happiness for
all, peace among us all, and comfort for all our
souls."

I said that this phrase had traditionally
been translated as "Learn from me, for I am
meek and humble of heart," and I believed
that the translation in our book was better. It
seems that in his own language Jesus used the
same word that Matthew had earlier trans-

lated as "poor in spirit" because he couldn't translate it into Greek with a single word. Here he translates it with other similar words. I think that the interpretation given here is very exact.

Because my yoke is soft
and my burden is light.

ALVARO: "His yoke is the only one that's not slavery but freedom: freedom from sin, freedom from oppression, freedom from everything. We've been talking here about simple people and humble people and poor people. It's them that Jesus calls to, to the ones who are tired of their burdens, so that they can find 'rest' in him—the solution to all their problems."

JULIO: "And the yoke he offers them is a new social system based on love. Their burden is to live together in a community of love, and that's a burden easy to bear. 'Submit to my liberation,' he's saying."

3.

The Wheat Gathered on the Sabbath

(Matthew 12:1–8)

We were in church for Sunday Mass. We read how, on the Sabbath, Jesus was walking in the country. His disciples were gathering wheat because they were hungry. And the Pharisees criticized Jesus, because it was a day of rest. He said to them:

> *Have you not read*
> *what David did on one occasion*
> *when he and his companions were hungry?*
> *He entered the house of God*
> *and ate of the sacred loaves,*
> *which neither he nor his companions*
> *   were allowed to eat,*
> *but only the priests.*

QUIQUE (a Puerto Rican law student) said: "Jesus makes them see that the laws, even the religious ones, should exist to serve people and not to oppress them. If a law makes people have to suffer hunger, that law is evil and must not be carried out. The lesson is not just

17

about the Sabbath. There are a lot of laws that make people suffer hunger, and we must do what Jesus did: disobey them."

OLIVIA: "The radio attacks the revolutionary priests, saying that they should devote themselves only to the administration of sacred things and that they shouldn't get mixed up in politics. The church should stay inside the temples, they say. But if that's the way it was it wouldn't accomplish anything. When Jesus tells the Pharisees that David ate those sacred loaves and that he was right to do so, he's telling them that religious things aren't sacred; it's people who are sacred."

ANTENOR (CHOP) said: "As I see it the gospel is against ritual. That's not important, Jesus is telling those religious people; what's important is people. And Jesus wants his church to be outside the temples, establishing justice in the world. And if at any time you have to do this through political action, that's where the priests should be and not in rituals or Masses or activities like that."

ELVIS: "Jesus is telling them that sin isn't to betray religious precepts, it's to betray people."

QUIQUE: "People are more important than laws, Jesus is teaching. But for the Christians of today as for the Pharisees of those times, it's just the opposite. Before birth-control pills became popular throughout the world the United States experimented with them on thousands of poor women in Puerto Rico. As a result of those experiments a great number of monstrous children were born. The church

protested, but not because of the monstrous
children nor because they were experi-
menting on poor people. It was because the
birth control was through pills and not
through some other method, for example,
rhythm. For them what was sacred was a law,
or rather a legality, not people."

> *Or have you not read in the law of Moses*
> *that the temple priests do not rest*
>   *on days of rest,*
> *and yet this is not a sin?*
> *Well I tell you that here*
> *there is something greater than the temple.*

TOMAS PEÑA: "You don't work to make
money but to help another Christian, and then
it's not a sin . . . "

His son FELIPE: "What's important, we're
shown here, is the fact that people are hungry
and not the religious laws. Jesus talks about
David and his companions being hungry. And
the gospel has also said that the disciples were
hungry. That's the way it was: The people
were hungry. They were hungry and they had
to break their own laws to eat the wheat, because they were hungry. It's like right now,
when you have to do something, like join a
movement, even though many people think
it's evil. The people are being screwed, the
people are suffering. It's more important to
make the revolution, it's urgent. That's why
he says to them: 'Here there is something
more important than the temple.' "

MARCOS: "The sin isn't to work Saturday or

Sunday or any other day. It's to exploit other people."

MANUEL: "And he tells them that the priests also work on a day of rest (and maybe they worked even more on those days because there were probably more sacrifices). And by this he wants to tell them that there shouldn't be differences between the priest and anyone else. Because the priests work in the temple, and why can't the others cut their wheat, then, if it's the same thing? So he's saying that all people are sacred."

DONALD: "That's clear, and that work could be as sacred as the temple work. And everything was temple and everybody was a priest."

ROMAN: "If you could make sacrifices on the Sabbath, you could do any other good thing."

FELIPE: "Unless it's a rich person making workers work to get more profit out of them."

LAUREANO: "Those bastards didn't realize that the commandment about the day of rest wasn't because it was a sin to work but so the workers could have a day of rest."

I said: "You're right. When God gave that commandment in Deuteronomy, he didn't give it as a religious precept but as a social precept. God tells them: 'You will do no work, neither you, nor your son, nor your daughter, nor your man servant, nor your woman servant, nor your ox, nor your ass, nor any of your animals, nor the stranger who dwells in your city; so that they may rest, like you, your man servant and your woman servant.' And afterwards he tells them that that is so that they will remember that once they had been slaves in

Egypt and that he had freed them. So the Sabbath was a commemoration of the liberation
and at the same time an announcement of the
future society in which there would be no slavery. If under the economic circumstances of
those times, people still could not eliminate
that way of production, at least they should
have one day of the week without slavery. This
was a step forward for Israel. Among the other
peoples of antiquity the servants worked
without interruption. Later it was also said in
the Bible that people must rest on the seventh
day just as God had rested from his creation.
By this they meant that just as people im-
itated God in creative work, so they should
imitate him in idleness. But here also they
spoke only of rest, not of ritual. Jesus recalled
the social character that the Sabbath had had,
and he made the Pharisees see that what had
been meant for liberation their ritualism had
converted into oppression. For in that very
passage about the wheat, he also said, according to Mark: 'The day of rest was made for
man, not man for the day of rest.' "

ADAN: "He is telling them that religion
shouldn't oppress people."

LAUREANO: "The trouble is that they
weren't interested in the worker. That's why
they had carried their religion to such stupid
extremes."

MANUEL: "They made the law just the opposite of what it was before, Jesus is saying. Instead of being used to lighten the work and the
burdens of the poor, now it's one more burden.
It prevents the poor from satisfying their

hunger if they're starving in the middle of a wheat field on a day of rest. As I see it those disciples were poor people, poor because they were starving there in the field. They didn't have even a nickel to buy anything. And the people that condemned them were of the upper classes, people who had a lot of food stored in their houses. And they didn't need to pull up sheaves in the field."

OLIVIA: "And Jesus puts more ideas in their heads by telling them that the temple isn't what's important now, that the community is what's sacred. That's why he'd been talking to them earlier about the temple, to tell them that now neither the consecrated loaves nor the priests nor the sacrifices—none of that counts. What is sacred is people."

FELIPE: "And also the priests should now say in the churches: 'Here there is something greater than the temple.' Because the revolution is more important than all religious things. But for many that's not the way it is: Religious ritual is more important than the people."

You have not understood
what the Scripture says:
"I want you to have love,
not to offer sacrifices."
If you understood it
you would not condemn innocent people.

CHOP: "This refers to a particular class, who must be the rich. And why? Well, because he tells them that their religion is no good as long as the people are being screwed."

I said: "Earlier he told them something very irreverent: that anybody can work on the Sabbath since the priests work on the Sabbath in their ritual. Now he tells them something more radical: that God wants not ritual but love among people. The phrase that he quotes is from the prophet Hosea, and here love means social justice, compassion for the poor. This is in line with all the prophets, who were always repeating that God wanted not ritual but a just society."

FELIPE: "They had the same mentality as capitalist people, who have no compassion for the poor, and who are always condemning simple people through the laws they impose on them. They are laws that are very sacred for them like, for example, the law of private property. But they are not laws that lead people to love each other or to unite or to live together in harmony. And so Jesus is telling those people that what they were teaching was drivel."

LAUREANO: "He's telling them they don't know shit about it, that they're talking because they have a pile of nonsense that isn't true in their heads, and that if they understood reality they wouldn't be condemning people."

OLIVIA: "It's not a question of changing the Sabbath for Sunday, or animal sacrifices for the sacrifice of the Mass. No, God doesn't want any ritual. God wants love and compassion for others."

I said: "He's telling them that he doesn't want religious sacrifices."

FELIPE: "He doesn't want false sacrifices."

I: "He doesn't say that he doesn't want *false* sacrifices; he doesn't want sacrifices. Period."

QUIQUE: "I think that when there is a just society, sacrifices will really mean something. Liturgy will be a true liturgy, and it will have a real meaning of communion with all people. But not until then."

LAUREANO: "Well, maybe then it won't be needed. And it won't be needed either if people always live in communion, everybody sharing the same goods: food, clothing, education, and all the rest—without any inequality or competition among people, in a continuous liturgy. There wouldn't be any need for liturgy because all of life would be a liturgy."

ELVIS: "He means then that communion isn't worth much now, right?"

QUIQUE: "Well, I don't think so. For me communion has a sense of solidarity with all human beings. I remember that sentence of Che when an old woman wrote him from Spain to ask if they could be relatives because she also was a Guevara. Che answered that he didn't know whether they belonged to the same Guevaras because his family had left Spain a long time ago, but if she felt as her own any injustice that was done anywhere in the world, well, then they were brother and sister. And I believe that's the meaning of the Eucharist, that receiving Jesus puts me in communion. That's the real justification for the church, I suppose, and that's why I became a convert. Christianity means that everybody is Jesus, everybody is part of this people, and what is mine you have to feel is yours."

CHOP: "Communion makes sense among those who are struggling for freedom, but not among the others."

QUIQUE: "As I see it, one part of the church is getting farther and farther away from the Bible every day. Where your treasure is, or your economic interests, there's where your mind is. When the Tupamaros sentenced to death that bandit named Mitrione, the Pope condemned them. But he hasn't said anything directly about Vietnam, only in general terms about peace and war. I'm more and more convinced that we have a great responsibility toward the world. I think that if the church had taught the true gospel there would have been no need for Communist parties anywhere. This is something that I've learned as a Christian: that you must get outside yourself. God wants a sacrifice, but it's the sacrifice of your own self. It's love."

CHOP: "But, you know, almost everywhere the leaders of the church are like those men who had no compassion for the hungry people who were cutting the sheaves. They also have forgotten that God doesn't want religious worship but love."

QUIQUE: "Like a picture we just saw in a magazine: Pinochet attending Mass in Brazil. That is totally useless. We saw the picture and I wondered what that priest celebrating the Mass could be telling him. He couldn't have been saying anything to him because there was no gospel he could be preaching to him. And Pinochet was standing, listening to him, with his bodyguards. I believe the same thing has happened to the church as to Israel: People inside the church falsified its doctrine, and people on the outside believed in it. And so now, even though some religious people are shocked, people outside the church are the ones who are practicing the gospels most and the ones who are most inspired by the Holy Ghost."

I said: "And now there are some new religious movements in Latin America that are limited to religious feelings. I think that this Christianity without politics is sometimes sponsored by the C.I.A."

Because the Son of Man has authority also over the day of rest.

MANUEL: "He has authority over rest and over work and everything else, including politics."

ANTENOR: "They had some laws that they themselves had invented and they made people believe that they were laws that came from God. Jesus takes away from them that authority that doesn't belong to them and he gives it to his people."

TOMAS said: "It's just as if on a Sunday, for example, I said: 'Today I'm not going to work, I'm going to rest.' And a bunch of people come to my house and I don't have any food to give them. And I say to myself: 'These people are my brothers and sisters.' And I go and get them some fish, some bananas. 'Look, eat!' And that's not a sin. Because people, since they are more important than the temple, are more important than the day of rest. And people decide whether to rest or to work on that day. That's the right that we have, as he's saying there."

I said: "The first Christians changed the Sabbath for Sunday because that was the day of the resurrection of Christ, but that was not to fulfill the ritualism of the Sabbath on another day. Not even to fulfill it with less legalism. Jesus did not answer the Pharisees that they were legalists and that to pull up a few sheaves was not work. From all that you have said here, I now see clearly that Jesus was more radical. He tells them that all work is sacred, that they are all priests, that people are more important than the temple, that religion ought to be at the service of people and not people at the service of religion, and finally that he has power to establish a new Sabbath, the definitive rest of humanity, when there will no longer be any alien work, when no servant will work for another person on any day of the week, when people's actions will be free like God's actions and their rest will be like God's rest. That new Sabbath that Christ came to establish on earth, represented among us now by Sunday, is the kingdom of freedom that will exist in the future. Saint Paul announced it saying: 'There will be a sacred rest for God's people; because those who go in to rest with God rest from their work as God rested from his.' "

4.

They Accuse Jesus of Having the Devil's Power

(Matthew 12:25–32)

We were in the meeting hut and we had had a lunch of rice and beans and fried pork (which Teresita served). This time we had with us my cousin Silvia and her husband, Alvaro, and my cousin Xavier and his wife, Sonia.

We had read that Jesus cured a man who had an evil spirit, and the Pharisees said that he had done it with the spirit of Beelzebub. And we went on to comment on what Jesus had said to them:

> *Any government that is divided into parties,*
> *and some fight against others, destroys it-*
> *self;*
> *and if a people or a family is divided,*
> *it cannot endure.*
> *So also, if Satan casts out Satan himself,*
> *he himself is divided;*
> *how, then, is his power going to endure?*

Someone said: "The devil, then, is like a government that's united, without divisions, like

28

in this government of Nicaragua everybody is united, made into a single body. Or like the National Guard. And that makes it terrible. That's something frightening: Evil is united like a single person."

OSCAR: "And this ought to be an example for us. Because if evil is united, we also must be united, with no divisions among us."

DON JOSE: "The devil is a united community. And we will defeat him only if we are a united community."

MARCELINO said: "But it's not a matter of setting one unity against another unity. The rich are united but united through selfishness, to defend their interests. The unity of the people cannot be like that. It must be a unity of love."

One of the girls: "We can cast out the devils if we are united by love."

And if I cast out the devils through
*   Beelzebub,*
through whom will your followers cast them
*   out?*
They themselves are contradicting you.

I said that this sentence of Jesus seemed to me puzzling. After a short silence, someone said: "It seems to me that Jesus is telling them that people in their group are not casting out devils. And the proof that they were on the devil's side was that they were not casting them out, because the devil is not divided. And so, now, people who defend this Nicaraguan regime, even though they are people high in

the church, they are the devil, because they
don't fight evil. They don't fight against injustice, which is the devil. And so we can find out
who's on whose side."

But I cast out the evil spirits
by means of the Spirit of God,
and this means that the kingdom of God
has now come to you.

MARCELINO: "God is love. And so that Spirit
of God is the Spirit of love. The devil is the
opposite of God and therefore the opposite of
love. He is selfishness. It's like two governments: God's and the devil's. And if the devils
are cast out, that means the kingdom of God is
already defeating the other one."

OSCAR: "And so the union of all of us, if we
are united by love, has to triumph over the
others who are united by selfishness."

I commented that it is generally considered
that the opposite of love is hatred, but I had
just read, in a book on the theology of liberation, exactly what Marcelino says, that the
opposite of love is selfishness. Hatred can exist
together with love and hatred can even inspire
love, or the opposite. But what is incompatible
with love is selfishness."

How then can someone enter the house
of a strong man
and take his things from him
if he does not first tie him up?
Only in this way can he take his things
from him.

JULIO MAIRENA: "The devil is united, but Christ conquered him. Here it says that the devil is a strong man but that Christ has tied him up."

Another young man: "And since he has tied him up, now he can take away his things. What are his things? The things he has stolen. They didn't belong to him, nothing belongs to him. Like an exploiter who is very rich but everything is stolen."

REBECA: "Here he's taking from the devil a person that he had possessed, but that person didn't belong to the devil and the devil had no reason to possess him. Christ comes to free all people possessed by the devil, that is, everybody possessed by selfishness."

ALVARO: "Jesus calls the devil a 'strong man.' It looks like he's a dictator."

I said that in Saint Luke's version of this same passage Jesus said that the strong man was well armed and that he disarmed him. It seems that when it speaks of "house" it isn't referring to a private house but to a fortress. Jesus entered the fortress of the strong man and took from him all his "things," that is, his armaments. He couldn't have done that, he said, if earlier he hadn't taken him prisoner. And so it's about the defeat of a tyrant."

We went on to the next verse, which seemed to have nothing to do with the preceding one:

He who is not with me is against me;
and he who does not help me gather scatters.

MARCELINO: " 'Gather' . . . 'scatter.' He's

talking about grain, the grains of a harvest, and we are the harvest. The gathered grain is all together. That's the community. The scattered grains are all over the place, far from each other. And therefore they are lost, they are useless. That happens with selfishness. That's why selfishness ruins us, casts us to the winds, separates us from each other. Love saves us, because it unites us."

Another said: "The devil is also a community, and it's also united but it's a community of disunion. It's united in order to scatter. Somebody said it's like the National Guard, but the Guard is united to divide the people, to oppress, to screw the people."

XAVIER: "There are only two governments. And each government is well united. Anyone who isn't with one government has to be with the other one. That's the way I see it."

I said that Jesus had said here: "He who is not with me is against me"; and that on another occasion when the disciples protested because a man was casting out evil spirits in his name without belonging to the group, he said to them: "He who is not against us is in our favor."

OSCAR: "That's very confused. But maybe I can untangle it. . . . " He repeated the two phrases of Jesus very slowly, again and again. He meditated a while. Then he said: "Well, in one case he says 'me' and in the other case 'us.' Maybe that's where the trouble is. First he says that anyone who isn't with him scatters. And it's because with Christ we unite others. Without him we have no love, and instead of uniting we divide. So in the Cooperative we can unite or else divide with gossip, envy, and quarrels. And afterward he says that anyone who isn't against us is with us. The one who isn't against us is the one who doesn't divide, who doesn't destroy the union. He's one of us. He's united. That's to say: the one who is not with unity is against Christ, and the one who is not against unity is with Christ."

I: "Can't you be neutral?"

OSCAR: "No. Because if you don't unite, for that very reason you're separating. Just not wanting to share in our unity is already a division. That's why anybody who isn't with Christ, who is the one who gathers us like grain, is separating us like a person casting the grain to the winds."

JULIO MAIRENA said: "He who isn't with him is against him; and he who isn't against him is with him. It's all the same."

Another said: "It's the opposite."

JULIO MAIRENA: "It's the opposite but it's the same." And he added after a pause: "I say that it's the same because anyone who doesn't love is selfish and is therefore a divider. And anyone who isn't selfish loves."

LAUREANO, his cousin: "You can also say: Anyone who isn't with the revolution is a counter-revolutionary, and anyone who's not against the revolution is a revolutionary."

WILLIAM: "Christ was not a fanatic or a totalitarian who said: 'He who is not a follower of mine I consider my enemy.' Let me explain: Che Guevara was not with him but he wasn't against him. Then, according to Christ, he was

with him. Che wasn't interested in being a
Christian because the only thing that interested him was fighting injustice, improving
the world. Then, according to Christ, he's a
Christian. As an example of someone who isn't
with him and therefore is against him, take
any bourgeois. That is, the person who really
isn't with him, who doesn't care about loving
others, doesn't care about changing the world,
that one is against him."

ALVARO: "I agree with William, and it seems
to me that you can also put it this way: the one
who isn't with him attacks him. But if somebody doesn't attack him, like that one who was
casting out devils without being his disciple,
then he's with him. Because if he weren't he'd
be attacking him."

I said: "And you can also say it this way:
Anyone who is not unjust is in favor of justice.
And anyone who is not in favor of justice (as
one might say, not in favor of the revolution),
that one is unjust, that one is for exploitation.
It's the opposite and it's the same, as Julio has
said."

And we went on to the last two verses, which
also didn't seem to have anything to do with
the preceding ones, and which were also very
mysterious:

> *Therefore I say to you*
> *that we can forgive people for all their sins*
> *and for all the evil they say;*
> *but if they blaspheme against the Holy Ghost*
> *they cannot be forgiven.*

And anyone who says anything against the
Son of Man will be forgiven;
but he who speaks offensive words against
the Holy Spirit will not be forgiven,
either in this world or in the other.

My cousin XAVIER asked me: "What do you
think is the sin against the Holy Spirit?"

And my cousin SILVIA: "In the first place,
who is the Holy Spirit?"

I asked if anyone had an answer, and after a
pause MARCELINO said: "I've heard in the
Creed that the Holy Spirit proceeds from the
Father and the Son. I've also read in a cate-
chism that I have at home that the Holy Spirit
is God the same as the Father and the Son.
Now, we know that God is love. What is it that
proceeds from God and is also God? It has to be
love. But if it proceeds it has to go somewhere.
Where? To us. Then that is the Spirit of love
that comes to us. What for? To stay here? No,
to proceed also from us out to others. The Holy
Spirit is, then, the same as the Spirit of unity
and love among us. Even though people reject
Christ, if they love others they are saved. But
if they refuse to love others, they won't be
saved in this world or in the other."

And ALVARO said: "It's wonderful how you
get so many reflections and such wise ones,
like those of the fathers of the church. I read
the Bible a lot all the time, and none of this
occurs to me. There's no doubt that the Holy
Spirit is among you. This Marcelino, for example, is a doctor of the church."

5.

The Parable of the Sower

(Matthew 13:1–13)

We were in the meeting hut. Opposite us the lake was calm as a mirror, with the stillness that it usually has on these May days. We had eaten rice and kidney beans and fish that Don Julio Guevara had caught. We now commented on the parable of the sower that Alejo read.

That day Jesus left the house
and sat at the edge of the lake.
As many people gathered where he was,
Jesus got into a boat and sat down,
and all the people stayed on the shore.
Then he taught them many things by means
*   of examples, saying:*
"A sower went out to sow . . ."

I said: "You are *campesinos* and you will be able to understand very well this parable of the seed that Jesus spoke from the boat. This parable is for you."

After a silence, MANUEL spoke, stammering a little: "The seed is tiny ... It seems to me that he means that the message of the king-

36

dom at the beginning is a small one, an insignificant one."

DON JOSE: "The seed is a living thing. You don't sow dead seeds. And so, as I see it, the message is a living thing."

OSCAR: "The seed is also something to eat. People sow grains that feed us. The words of Jesus are grains that he scatters in the wind, to feed us all."

"The seed is a single thing and it becomes many things," said MARCELINO.

Another: "The seed is a tiny, wrinkled, ugly thing, and anyone who doesn't know better might think that it's useless. And it's the same with the word of God, it seems to me, when the person that receives it doesn't know what it contains."

WILLIAM, with his son Juan in his arms, said: "And there's another special thing about the seed, as I see it. It's not only a living thing but it's the transmission of life."

"We are all seeds. Seeds who produce more seeds," said NATALIA, who was the midwife.

OSCAR: "Christ rose from the dead because he was a healthy seed. In the harvest we have seen that not every seed is born but only the good seeds, the nice, healthy ones. And so, if we're going to rise from the dead like Christ we must be of the same kind of seed that he was. If we're a dead seed, a vain seed, or as we say a seed 'with the evil eye,' we won't rise from the dead. Because we've been dead for some time, we have 'the evil eye,' it seems to me."

I said: "The seed has to be buried and die to

be able to be born. This is the other great mystery of the seed."

And OLIVIA said: "I think that Jesus spoke of the seed because he was talking for us *campesinos* and not for the rich. If he had been talking for the rich he would have used examples that they would have understood very well. But he used this example of the seed because he was talking our language. He was talking about seeds and birds that eat the grains and of plants that die of oversoaking and of swamps, because that's our language and because the message is for us poor people."

TOMAS: "And when we hear the message and we forget it, it's like the corn that the birds ate. You sow now, and tomorrow when you go to look there's nothing at all. The birds ate it all. The birds are the devil that carried off the message that had been sown."

His son FELIPE: "That seed fell near the road, where the ground was walked on, because everybody passes by there. That's what happens with people who have their minds closed by propaganda. They're walked on, they believe what everybody tells them, and then the message of the kingdom doesn't get through to them. They receive the message if they come here, but they go home and they forget it as soon as they turn on the radio."

OSCAR: "Another seed fell among stones. The rocky ground is the hard heart, where there is a lot of selfishness and little love. The message doesn't take root in a heart where there is little love."

I said that another seed was smothered by the thorns, which, according to Christ, are the cares of this world and the seduction of riches, and I told them what I once heard Thomas Merton say that it is interesting to observe that for Christ riches are not sweet and pleasant; they are thorns.

MARCELINO: "This seems very clear to me."

I asked why it was very clear. And he said: "They are thorns. The thorns are tiny. They get into our skin and they're very annoying. If the thorns weren't so small they couldn't break the skin. So, riches are very insignificant and therefore they bother you a great deal. When you have something in you which doesn't belong there, it's very painful. And the more delicate the thing that's in you the more it hurts and the harder it is to take out. And you walk around with riches like somebody who has a tiny, tiny palm thorn in each heel, which will scarely let you walk."

CESAR: "To be rich is to be bothered."

But another portion fell on good ground
and gave a good harvest;
some of the plants gave a hundred grains for
*   each seed,*
others sixty grains,
and others thirty.
If you have ears, listen!

MARCELINO: "These words about the seed that we are hearing here are that same seed, and maybe we hadn't realized it. If we hear these words the seed of the kingdom is buried in us, he says. But he speaks of the kingdom only for those who have ears."

FELIX MAYORGA: "Sometimes the word of Jesus sprouts and sometimes it doesn't. That's what we've been told here."

MANUEL: "As I see it, in this harvest a lot of seed is lost, maybe most of it. But in the end the seeds that produce make up for all that loss. That's what I believe will happen with the harvest of these words. The good people, who now are very few, will be a great society, because each one will become a lot."

JULIO: "I see one thing. The seed alone, without the land, doesn't do anything. So this doctrine without us is of no use. Without us there is no kingdom of heaven."

OLIVIA: "From that boat in a cove he was sowing there for them. And now in this group he's sowing too."

I said: "At the beginning we saw that 'Jesus left the house and sat at the edge of the lake.' Quite often the gospels speak of '*the* house' without saying what it is. It seems that these are remains of the memory of a certain house that was very familiar to them. As a detail, it says that the lake was near. Jesus probably lived there with his community, or he had his center of operations there. He doesn't appear teaching in the synagogues but in a kind of open-air school. Perhaps he left the synagogues in disgust, or more probably he was expelled. With the parable of the sower there begins a series of parables known as the

'Sermon of the Lake,' which were probably not the teachings of one day but of a long time. Matthew shows us Jesus seated, and perhaps that's because teachers taught classes that way. But Jesus isn't sitting in his chair in a classroom but in a boat. And the teachers taught their classes to a select group of students, but Jesus isn't teaching an elite but the whole town. These lessons of the lake are simple examples taken from daily life, because, as Olivia has said very well, he is talking for the simple people. It seems as though Jesus has already realized that the only ones that follow him are the simple people."

> *Then the disciples approached Jesus and*
>   *asked him:*
> *"Why do you speak to people by means of*
>   *examples?"*
> *He answered them:*
> *"God lets you know the secrets of the king-*
>   *dom of heaven,*
> *but they cannot know them."*

WILLIAM: " 'They' are the powerful and the rich. Now it is clear that Jesus is keeping a secret with his people; it seems that those courses he's giving are a little bit underground. He has seen the reaction that his preaching has aroused in other circles. A bad atmosphere has grown up for him, and he sees repression coming. So this business of talking about the kingdom by means of parables is also a strategy."

MARCELINO: "But he says he really is revealing his secret to others." And lowering his voice a little: "It's interesting to know that the kingdom of God is a secret. It's announced to many people, but always in secret. And also it's a thing that's there, but it's hidden. Like a seed that's buried, that isn't seen."

Because to him who has, more shall be given,
and he will have enough;
but from him who has not
will be taken away even the little that he has.

MANUEL said: "I've observed that when a rich farmer sows two thousand acres of cotton, with a lot of machinery, with insecticide, with herbicide, with fertilizer and all the rest, he earns a lot of money. He was already very rich and now he gets richer. On the other hand the poor man who has nothing sows two acres and it doesn't turn out well, and at the end of the harvest he's in debt and poorer than before. So even the little he had the bank takes away from him."

OSCAR: "Yes, that happens with money, and the gospel doesn't refer to money but to love. But it seems that Jesus is saying to us that in his kingdom a similar thing happens as with money. Since money attracts more money, so love attracts more love. And since all the deals of a rich man turn out well, especially if he's very rich, so the person who has much love is given much more love by God. But God takes from the selfish person who exploits others even the little bit of good that he had in his heart. And if he was evil before now he turns more evil until he becomes completely evil. Because selfishness attracts more selfishness as love attracts more love."

This is why I speak to you through examples;
because they see and remain as if they did
*   not see;*
they hear and remain without understand-
*   ing,*
as if they did not hear.

ALEJANDRO: "The examples of Jesus are very clear for simple people. They say nothing to proud people, who despise this language of Jesus because it is simple. For some it's a revelation; for others it's an enigma. It's so simple that only the simple understand it."

LAUREANO: "He came so that some people would believe in him and others wouldn't. And now it's the same with the revolution. Some accept it and others have to reject it. If everybody accepts it then it's not a revolution."

MARCELINO: "The parables of Jesus have a double effect: Some people understand them, and people who shouldn't understand them don't."

I asked if this was clear and several said: "It's clear."

SILVESTRE exclaimed: "Now it's very clear."

6.

The Wheat and the Weeds

(Matthew 13:24–30, 36–43)

Jesus told us that the kingdom of heaven is like a man who sowed wheat. An enemy sowed weeds among the wheat. The slaves urged him to pull up the weeds, but he said to them:

No, because in pulling up the weeds,
you can also pull up the wheat.
Better let them grow together
until the harvest;
and then I shall order the workers
to gather first the weeds
and tie them in bundles to burn them,
and afterwards to store the wheat in my
  granary.

I said that last Sunday we heard the parable of the sower. In this other parable Christ told us that in reality there are two sowers: the sower of wheat and the sower of weeds. Because in the world there is not only good. There is good and evil.

OLIVIA: "But the good comes only from one

44

of the sowers. The evil comes from the other one, his enemy."

FELIPE: "What I see here is that humanity is divided into two classes: the ones who do good and the ones who do injustice. Some are from one sower, and the others from the other."

PANCHO: "And we also see here that good and evil are not separate but together. Justice is well mixed with injustice. Don't tell me now, for example, that all the poor are the good ones and all the rich are the evil ones."

MARCELINO: "Of course not. We have a world in which good and evil are mixed together. Now there's no reason to say that everything is good or that everything is evil. But one day they'll be separated, all the good on one side and all the evil on the other. One to be gathered, the other to be destroyed."

FELIX: "As a sower I know from experience that the weed is more resistant; the good plant is delicate. That's why we can't pull up the weeds until the other plant is strong. That's what happens now with injustice, which is stronger than justice. We have to hope that at first justice will develop more."

JULIO: "As I see it, God is a good *campesino* who knows how to cultivate his field. The peons, on the other hand, were not very expert."

ALEJANDRO: "An interesting thing: First they're going to destroy the evil. Only afterwards will they harvest the good."

OSCAR: "I find here that God allows us to do

what we feel like. He lets time go by so that the good and the evil grow equally, because that evil may be good afterwards and if he pulls it up too soon he doesn't give people a chance to change."

OLIVIA: "We have evil inside us, too, and if God tore it out right away he would tear us out, too. We are good and evil. Good in some things and evil in others."

And a boy who was visiting us, who was a delinquent in Managua and is now rehabilitated: "There are a lot of people who are evil, but you can teach them to be good and you can make them change. And so God gives us this chance, as Oscar says."

Another said: "Right now you can't separate evil and good completely without destruction. You can do it only by force."

OSCAR: "You can't do it, man. You pull up the weeds, and maybe you're pulling up the best. Because with time that bad plant can get better. God knows that you can begin bad and end up good, just as the good is good now but can end up bad. So God can't pull up any plant. He has to let them grow and with time he's going to choose."

FELIPE: "Maybe we ourselves will later have better judgment and will know which of us are the evil ones and which are the good ones. And then we ourselves could choose, don't you think?"

OSCAR answers: "That's at the end of time, according to the gospels, when we'll be able to separate the good from the evil in the world."

A Venezuelan hippie: "We often reject injustice, but we fall into another injustice. We break away from the system, but we create other systems. It's a good thing to know that a day will come when justice and injustice will be totally separate, and from then on there'll only be justice."

I said that we have always tended to believe that all the good is on one side and all the evil on the other, even though the time for such a separation hasn't come. Christians have also often believed that they were the only good people, and that all the others were evil. But the church from the beginning began to see that evil was also flowering within itself. It must have been at that time that in the Christian community they began to remember and repeat this parable that they had heard Christ tell and that later was put into the written gospel. The lesson of this parable is very clear: Good and evil are united now in the present and they will be separated in the future.

HORACIO: "And right now I believe evil is winning out over good because there's so much injustice. Even though it's true we're fighting against that injustice, and that's what the gospel is telling us here."

ALBERTO: "But the separation won't happen until the other life. Because it says that it will be done by the angels."

We went on then to read the interpretation of the parable, which Christ himself gave in private to the disciples when they reached the house:

The harvest represents the end of the world,
and those who gather the harvest
are the angels.
Just as the weeds are gathered
and thrown on the fire to be burned,
so it will happen at the end of the world.
The Son of Man will order his angels
to gather up from his kingdom
all the scandalmakers and the evildoers.
They will cast them into the fiery furnace,
where there will be weeping
and gnashing of teeth.
Then the just will shine like the sun
in the kingdom of his Father.
If you have ears, listen!

FELIPE: "It seems to me that the angels must just be people who are going to separate the good from the evil. God's going to do this through people. People have been good by nature. Evil is not of our nature; it was brought to us from outside. And God's going to make use of us, too, in fixing up that crop. Because it would be an error to believe that God is going to fix up the world without counting on us."

I said that the word "angels" means "messengers." God appears in the Bible always acting through messengers, and these are the angels. It seems to me very natural that these angels or messengers of the Son of Man, of whom Christ speaks here, should be people, as Felipe says, who are going to separate good from evil. As for the harvest being the end of the world, as Christ says, it seems to me that it means that it's the end of evil, not the end of the universe. Because what's the good of ending evil if you also end the universe? Christ speaks of a harvest, and that harvest cannot be a destruction. He also speaks of an annihilation by fire, but that refers only to the weeds.

I also said that I believe, like José Porfirio Miranda, that the Last Judgment is going to come in this world (the complete fulfillment of justice on earth), which, however, does not exclude a survival after death. In the gospels we're told that the judgment began in history at the time of Christ. And the Apostle Saint James tells us that the judgment is for the rich.

LAUREANO: "I believe when we eliminate the exploitation of people by people we're going to have something like grass separated from weeds."

ELVIS: "It seems to me that we're beginning to see that separation in several countries, in Cuba, for example. It's at least a beginning."

OSCAR: "I believe that the gathering of wheat in the granary is the union of humankind. The bad plants are those that have been followers of separation, and those are going to be cast out."

I said: "Jesus says that all the 'scandalmakers' and the evildoers will be gathered up first. 'Scandal' is a word that comes from the Greek and means a stumbling stone. In the Bible the word indicates a causer of injustice, and not what we mean today by the word 'scandal.' Jesus is saying here that they are going to remove all the obstacles (that is, those opposed to unity) and those who do evil."

LAUREANO interrupted me: "It's like saying the reactionaries."

I also said that the image of the fiery furnace is to tell us that evil will be annihilated. And the weeping and gnashing of teeth gives the idea that it's something that stays outside.

MARCELINO: "Wheat is used to make bread. The evil plant serves its own purposes, to bear its useless fruit that is no good for people. The evil person is the one who serves only himself and not the rest of humankind. That's why he's evil."

I said that Jesus compares them to the "just," that is, those who have done justice. And he says that "they will shine like the sun," which seems to me indeed to be a reference to resurrection: a transformation of our substance.

ELVIS: "But I think we can speed up the coming of the harvest and of the gathering in the granary, if we start now to be just."

TERESITA: "It's very clear now. The wheat and the weeds are those who love and those who don't love."

WILLIAM: "Or the revolutionaries and the non-revolutionaries."

Someone asked me why he says, "If you have ears, listen." I said that Jesus often says that after a parable, because it's up to us to understand it or not, according to our disposition. We can hear this story that Jesus tells us like someone who hasn't listened to a word, or else these words can penetrate into us and transform our lives. To have ears is to be ready to receive this message, and that's the same as being ready to receive the kingdom.

7.

The Mustard Seed and the Yeast

(Matthew 13:31–35)

The kingdom of heaven is like a mustard seed
that a man sowed in his field.
It is certainly the smallest of all seeds,
but when it grows
it becomes the largest of plants
and gets to be a tree,
so big that the flying birds
come to make nests in its branches.

MANUEL: "It seems to me that the word of God is a very delicate thing, very tiny. At first it seems insignificant and therefore many people despise it, but afterwards it grows like a mustard tree. And so at first Jesus spoke his word to twelve people, and that was very insignificant, but it spread to others and was scattered throughout the world. And it has spread so far it has reached even us in Solentiname. It also seems to me that the word of God is tiny and insignificant because it sprouts in our hearts and you almost can't see it. But then I tell it to someone else, and so it grows and spreads like a great tree, and this tree is the transformation of the world."

DOÑA ADELA, a little old lady, said: "We who

are here have seen that little seed growing."

I asked what that "kingdom of heaven" was that Jesus compared with the mustard seed.

NATALIA answered energetically: "It seems to me that the kingdom of heaven is unity. When all of us join together and all of us love each other, that will be the kingdom of God."

I said it was strange that for so long people believed that the kingdom of heaven was in heaven. And even today many educated Christians continue to believe this. The fact is that it was easier to think of the kingdom in the other world so as not to have to change this one. We know that Matthew used the word "heaven" because of the Jewish custom of not saying the word "God." If the kingdom of God were heaven, there would be no sense to all those parables about the kingdom: that the kingdom of heaven is like a net that catches good and bad fish, that it's like a field in which there is wheat mixed with weeds, that it's like a buried treasure, that it's like a seed, that it's like yeast.

And there would be no sense to another parable, found in one of the apocryphal gospels but apparently an authentic one: The kingdom of heaven is like a woman who carries a bowl of flour home without noticing that the bowl is broken, and when she gets home she finds that all the flour is gone. I said also that this last parable is like an image of the church, compromised by power and money, preferring to think of the kingdom only in the other life and not in this one. And therefore now that hu-

manity is on the point of making bread (trans-
forming the world), the church has lost all the
flour. Jesus told Pilate that his kingdom was
not of this world, but by this he meant that it
was in contrast to all the other political king-
doms, because it was not a kingdom of power.
This kingdom, as Natalia has said very well, is
union, love.

WILLIAM said: "That's why he compares it
with a mustard seed. Because instead of a
kingdom of worldwide power, which the Jews
were waiting for (which was a reactionary
idea), the kingdom of Jesus is shown as a very
humble little group, which goes unnoticed at
the beginning: a carpenter with a few poor
people. Among his disciples he didn't have one
important person. Later it will also be a political kingdom that will control the earth, and
that's why he says it will be greater than all
the trees. But at the beginning it was an invis-
ible kingdom."

And TERESITA, William's wife, with her son
Juan in her arms, said: "The truth is that the
kingdom belongs to the poor, and that's why
it's unnoticed at first. But the poor will control
the world and will possess the earth."

LAUREANO: "And you can say the same
about the revolution: at the beginning nobody
notices it. It's little groups, cells."

The poet CORONEL URTECHO, who was visiting us, said: "Like this little group now that's
telling us these things in Solentiname." And
he added, after a pause: "On the other hand,
there are ostentatious works of the church,

created with great pride, that give promise of being great things, and end up in nothing. They are the opposite of the kingdom of God, like the Jesuit Central-American University."

LAUREANO: "And the guerrilla groups are small, insignificant, poor. And they're often wiped out. But they're going to change society. Can't we apply also to them the parable of the mustard seed?"

MARCELINO, with his calm voice, said: "I don't know about the mustard seed, but I do know about the *guasima* seed, which is tiny. I'm looking at that *guasima* tree over there. It's very large, and the birds come to it too. I say to myself: that's what we are, this little community, a *guasima* seed. It doesn't seem there's any connection between a thing that's round and tiny, like a pebble, and that great big tree. It doesn't seem either that there's any connection between some poor *campesinos* and a just and well-developed society, where there is abundance and everything is shared. And we are the seed of that society. When the tree will develop we don't know. But we know that we are a seed and not a pebble."

I said: "The great tree with all its branches and its leaves is already present in the seed, even though in a hidden form. In the same way the kingdom of heaven, which is a cosmic kingdom, is already present in us, but in a hidden way. A tree is the product of the evolution of a seed, and in nature everything is produced by a process of evolution. And it seems to me that with this parable of the seed Christ is also telling us here that the kingdom of heaven is the product of the same process of evolution that formed stars, plants, animals, people. And it grows in us impelled by the same forces of nature that impelled the evolution of the whole cosmos, which is to say that the kingdom of heaven is evolution itself."

ELVIS: "The birds that make their nests in the branches, it seems to me, are humanity now free: people who can go freely everywhere without borders of any kind and who will feel safe in the universe, without any of them ever being in need."

TERESITA: "This parable also teaches us that we must be patient, because a tree isn't created in a single day, and all the processes of nature take their time."

OLIVIA: "The kingdom of heaven or the kingdom of love begins with a tiny bit. When we work on it, that seed grows and grows."

"I've seen that seed growing here, blessed be God," said DOÑA ADELITA in her faint voice.

OLIVIA continued: "The kingdom of heaven is also taking shape in our homes with the growing children that we are shaping. They are growing up, and the kingdom of love is taking shape, which is the kingdom of heaven. It has to take shape in a child. And then it goes on developing, and if the children develop well they are going to extend that kingdom of love also. Yes, you can notice also how the kingdom of heaven is growing inside the child."

He also gave them this other example:
The kingdom of heaven is like the yeast
that a woman puts into three measures
   of flour,
to make all the dough ferment.

MANUEL: "It's the same thing. Because the yeast is also small and makes all the dough grow."

I asked what the dough was, and he answered very emphatically: "Everybody!"

I said: "So the yeast is the love that there is in humanity. At the beginning it may have seemed small, insignificant. We still see it quite small inside ourselves, but it grows and develops, and it is going to unite us all."

LAUREANO: "In the book we're reading now in the Youth Club we've seen how revolutionary groups have acted as catalysts for the people. That's like being the yeast of the people."

DOÑA ADELITA: "Faith is the yeast."

ELVIS: "The yeast comes out of the people themselves. But at the beginning it's a little group and it makes the dough grow. Without the yeast the dough doesn't grow and there's no bread."

CESAR: "The kingdom of heaven is love, and therefore Jesus says it's like a seed that a man sows on his land and like yeast that a woman puts in the dough. Because it's the love that God has put in us, so that it will grow."

ELVIS: "It almost comes to the same thing.

The two things are tiny at first and afterwards they grow."

I said: "And this is also so that we won't be discouraged. Here we see that our group is tiny. Many people are afraid to come. But Jesus tells us that the kingdom of heaven begins with something very tiny. You have to remember that this little group is also a ferment inside its dough."

DONALD: "In many places there is yeast that breaks things apart."

I: "What Donald says is quite true, and Christ also somewhere else tells us to be wary of 'the yeast of the Pharisees and the yeast of Herod,' because evil is also a little group, an elite that corrupts all the dough. The yeast of the Pharisees seems to be the corruption of the religious elites, and the yeast of Herod the corruption of the power elites. He spoke that warning after the multiplication of the loaves. . . "

FELIPE interrupted me: "And here too he's talking about bread. Why does Jesus give bread as an example? It seems to me that it's because bread is a material reality (although it's not only material), because we have to fulfill love in a material way: by means of food, drink, clothing, housing, and all the other things produced by nature and the work of people. That's why Jesus uses that materialistic parable."

I said that in fact the kingdom of heaven is to

satisfy hunger, all of our hunger, naturally including all the material necessities. And that's why Jesus compares it with a loaf that is going to be baked; and the yeast that will make it grow is love. I also said that on the eve of the French Revolution, when the first signs of popular uprising were beginning to be seen, the revolutionaries in Paris were saying: "The bread is rising." They were referring to the mass of the people who were rising up, but they also saw it as a mass of flour. And the revolution was the great loaf of bread. We can still say that the bread is rising wherever the people are rising. It's the whole universe that is rising impelled by evolution and revolution, until it reaches its perfection, which is the kingdom of heaven, as Saint Matthew says, or the kingdom of God, as the other evangelists say, or the kingdom of love. And this is also the same eucharistic bread that we raise up at the altar, "Which earth has given and human hands have made," as we say in the Offertory. We offer it to God as a representation of all the fruits of earth and of work.

ALEJANDRO: "And this bread is to be shared by everyone. That's why the miracle of the multiplication of the loaves was also another teaching: to teach us to share the bread."

CESAR: "The flying birds go all over the place, right? They don't have any nests. Those birds who didn't have any place to live reach the tree and find a place to be. They have a nest. Now we're told one more thing about the kingdom of heaven: that it's like a loaf of bread that takes away your hunger."

DOÑA ADELITA: "When I begin to bake a loaf of bread, it's God who makes it grow for me. I say to myself: 'Oh, what am I going to do to make it grow!' And would you believe? It grows. And it's the same way with my love for God every day: Will it grow? And it grows more and more."

LAUREANO: "The only thing I would say is that we've got to play the part assigned to us, as a seed that's going to grow and not a seed that produces nothing. And as a good yeast that makes the bread rise."

WILLIAM: "There are two little words here that we must notice: The woman *put* the yeast in three measures of flour, and so she made *all* the dough ferment. This means, in the first place, that we have to mix in with all the dough, get inside it and make ourselves one with it. In the second place, it means that it's the total mass that is called on to ferment, it's with all people that the loaf is going to be formed. And this is what 'Catholic' means: universal. This church has this name because it's not one more religion, separated from the other religions. Its goal is the unity of the totality of people, the creation of the Universal Person."

The poet CORONEL said: "And why three measures of grain? Why not two—or four?"

Some of us smiled. We didn't answer. And he repeated: "Surely that was the quantity that the women of that time were accustomed to mix, three measures. Like saying now an *arroba* of flour. But I think that maybe there is something more than that."

I told him to tell us.

CORONEL: "The Trinity. The Trinity, which is the mystery of the love of God, of the community of God: the Father, the Son, and the Holy Spirit. And also the love of the family: William and Teresita with Juan, who has been born to them and who is the son. The three measures, then, must be the love of two people who produce a third. The fruitfulness of love that always engenders love."

LAUREANO said: "In Cuba the Communist Party is considered to be a vanguard that makes the whole mass advance. And it really is an elite of the most sacrificing and most revolutionary people, and in that sense you can say that it also is a yeast."

PANCHO: "We're talking about the gospel, not about Communism. . . "

I said that in Cuba Christianity had turned out the opposite of the way Christ had wanted. It had been a Christianity of dough and not of yeast. Whereas the yeast there had been Communism.

CORONEL, turning to me: "With regard to Christianity and Communism, some thoughts on the subject occurred to me recently and I intended to tell them to you, and I'll tell them now to the whole community. Here they are: Communism cannot absorb Christianity without ceasing to be completely Communist and changing into Christianity, whereas Christianity can absorb Communism (Marxism-

Leninism) and continue to be Christianity and
even be more Christian. To put it another way,
the Communist cannot become a convert to
Christianity without ceasing to be exclusively
Communist and becoming a Christian,
whereas the Christian can become a Communist (Marxist-Leninist) and be even more of
a Christian."

We went on to the last verses, in which it is
said that Jesus spoke only in parables, in order
to fulfill what the prophet had said:

I shall speak by means of examples;
I shall say things that have been secret
since God made the world.

Nobody made any other commentary, and I
said: "The kingdom of heaven has been gradually taking shape since the beginning of the
world. First it has been slowly developing with
the very slow evolution of the universe and
afterwards, more swiftly, with the revolutions
of human society. But neither nature nor
human beings knew where all this was leading, until Christ came to reveal it. The secret of
evolution and of revolution (of the universe
and of people) it seems to me is that secret that
was hidden from the beginning of the world.
Christians are not necessarily more revolutionary or more loving than non-Chris-
tians. But the Christians, as one of the Latin
American theologians of liberation has said,
are *the ones who know*. They know, through
the gospel, where the revolution is going,

and what the goal of love is. And Christ is now revealing that secret hidden from the beginning of the world here to this little group in Solentiname."

And I said afterwards that Christians and Communists had always believed that Christianity and Communism were opposed to each other, but recently the gospel itself has revealed to us what the poet Coronel has just said: that the Christian can become a Communist and be even more of a Christian. And this is also a truth that up to now had been hidden.

8.

The Hidden Treasure

(Matthew 13:44)

We next had a very brief parable:

The kingdom of heaven is like a treasure
hidden in a plot of ground.
A man finds the treasure
and hides it again right where it was,
and filled with joy he goes and sells
  all that he has
and he buys that plot of ground.

I began by saying that this example has a
good deal of current significance for us, now
that many archeological treasures are being
found in Solentiname: at the Ortegas, on Don
Catucho Guadamuz's property, and on
Juana's island.

And FELIPE said: "We already know that the
kingdom of heaven is the kingdom of love.
Then love is what is like a treasure for us. Love
forces us to get rid of selfishness and sell all
our possessions."

ALEJANDRO: "To sell everything in order to

63

buy the plot of land with the treasure means to
get rid of everything we have in order to be
able to love. Because if you have and don't give
what you have, you don't love the others because you don't share what you have with the
others. When you have love, when you make
friendships, when you unite with others, you
have found that treasure."

Another of the boys said: "I believe now it
has all been said. Love is giving yourself to
others. If not, it's a love that's not secure, it's
deceiving yourself. But it seems to me that
depends on what you have. Some people who
are poor like us, how can we buy that treasure?
Well, only with love because that's all we have
to offer. People who have more to give, they
have more obligations."

I said: "The gospel says that the man sold
everything he had. The kingdom of heaven always demands that of us. Those who have little must get rid of the little that they have, and
those who have much must get rid of the much
that they have. But everybody must get rid of
everything. That man was left with nothing,
and only in that way could he acquire that
treasure."

OSCAR: "But the man who found that treasure, what did he do with it afterwards? Did he
give it away?

MANUEL: "No, he wanted it for himself, to
enjoy it himself. But the things he owned before he didn't want anymore, because he preferred to exchange them for the treasure. And
Jesus gives us that as an example. That's what

we must do with all the things we have, exchange them all for love in order to enjoy that love."

I said that there was a detail in this little parable that we also should notice: the joy of the man who sells everything he has to buy the plot of ground.

REBECA said: "It's like a community where love exists. There is a lot of joy in it, because everyone loves everyone. It's all one unity. It seems to me that's the treasure. And that's the joy that there is."

I said that we must also notice another detail: the treasure was hidden. And REBECA said again: "Because selfishness is much more plentiful than love. But where there's love there's joy. Where there's selfishness there's no love. People don't love each other and they can't help each other."

FELIPE: "It seems to me it's like Doña Rebeca says. It seems to me too that it's a hidden treasure, because just now we've discovered this and we understand it. The gospel is like a hidden treasure because nobody used to understand it, right? They used to read it to us in Latin, and they preached on it in a way that wasn't even close to the true gospel. And now we're discovering it, as you might say: we're finding a treasure. But in order to possess it, we have to exchange all we have for love, to fill ourselves with love. If we don't, even though we've discovered the gospel, we don't possess it."

TOMAS, Felipe's father: "It seems to me that

when a town is all alone and doesn't have anyone there to teach the gospel, and somebody
comes to teach it, it's like that community has
discovered a treasure, and it's a joy for everyone."

OSCAR: "I believe all of us who come to this
Mass have the good luck to discover that
treasure, because we really are discovering
it."

JULIO: "After all, this example that Jesus
gives here is an example about money. What
this man made was a business deal. Why does
Jesus give this example? It seems to me it's
because people always want to have more and
more and more money. And what we ought to
want to have is more and more love."

I said that this also was a very intimate
experience, and that's why it was compared to
a hidden treasure. And there's another detail
in Jesus' little story: the man who discovered
the treasure hid it again. So also the kingdom
of heaven, though later it will be a social reality, is now hidden inside us. It is within us, in
the deepest part of our being, that each one of
us can find it.

I asked if anyone had anything to add.

Someone added: "I think we're finding
it . . . "

9.

The Net

(Matthew 13:47–52)

We were in the meeting hut. The lake was
slightly rippled by the south wind. The boats
bobbed, tied to the little wooden dock. We had
had lunch and now we were commenting on a
short parable. LILIAM, Marcelino's beautiful
daughter, had read:

> *The kingdom of heaven is also like a net*
> *that is cast into the sea*
> *and it gathers up all kinds of fish,*
> *and when it is full*
> *they bring it up on the shore,*
> *and there they sit down to sort them,*
> *and they put the good fish in baskets*
> *and they throw away the bad fish.*

OLIVIA: "The kingdom of heaven will be established here on earth. It is love and justice
among people. As we see in this parable, now
good and evil are mixed up. But a day will come
when the sorting will take place and only the
good will be left, the good part of humanity."

ALEJANDRO, her son: "This sorting will take

place here, and I don't believe that God will have to send in the angels for that. He's going to do it through people, through a social change. And I think that from now on we can begin that purging of ourselves, of our society. We too are those same fishermen who have caught those fish."

MARCELINO: "As I see it there are two humanities: the one that's existed so far, which is the dragnet one, with good and bad fish, and the one that'll come afterwards, which will be a true community, the community of the basket. The fish that are no good don't form any community, they aren't in any basket, they are cast out. I think that the basket of good fish is love. The fish cast out are people who remain in selfishness, in individualism."

OSCAR: "Yes, because selfishness and love can't stay together. Just as good fish and bad fish can't go to market. Even though, to catch them, you do cast the net for whatever it drags in, and the sorting comes afterwards. The Lord must have done some fishing at times when he was with fishermen, and he knew something about the operation."

I said: "And he was also talking to fishermen like Julio Guevara, Tomás Peña, the Altamiranos, the Madrigals, and María Peña. This is the last parable of the so-called Sermon of the Lake, which he spoke on the shores of the Lake of Galilee, a lake like this one. Beside the lake was that house where Jesus lived, mentioned in the Gospels. And in that lake was the miraculous catch. There he walked on the waters. There he calmed the storm. There he preached from a boat. And also on those shores he appeared to them afterwards resurrected. I think that at the time of this parable he was perhaps watching some boats on the shore, as we are watching them now. Perhaps he was watching some dragnet, and it was then that he said for them and for us: 'The kingdom of heaven is like a dragnet . . . ' "

DON JULIO GUEVARA: "And we are those fish too . . . "

DON TOMAS PEÑA, who is also a good fisherman like Don Julio: "A comparison isn't the same thing, it's something similar. So the kingdom of heaven is like a dragnet that catches all kinds of fishes, like the book says. But there's a difference, as I understand it. The fishes that are caught in the net aren't to blame if they're bad, if they're of no use to us. On the other hand, the people who are in the net of the kingdom of heaven *can* choose to be what we are. And there's no need for angels coming to do the sorting because we've already done it ourselves. We can be *moga* or *roncador*, *machaca* or *guapote*. The beach has all kinds of fish: there's a *mojarra*, those white *palometas* that are very good *mojarras*, the *guapote*, the *róbalo*, the *roncador* are very good fish. And there are others that aren't eaten, like the *moga*, which is *alaste* and has a smell of dirt because it eats only dirt, the *cartilla* which is skinny, skinny, nothing but bones, and the *beata*, which when it's fried has no taste and is half rotten. But on that other shore that is mentioned there, it's up to us to be good fish or bad fish, it seems to me."

WILLIAM: "It says that the net is pulled in 'when it is full,' which means that they have to take their time. And this explains why good and bad are now mixed up everywhere, even in the church. The time for pulling in the net hasn't come yet. But this also means that not all time is going to be like that. Afterwards only the good will be left. The rest will be thrown out."

"And I think this will come rather soon," I said. "First, because certain historic signs are beginning to be seen, what Jesus calls the 'signs of the times.' And second because Jesus always insisted that all this that he was announcing, the kingdom of heaven, was 'near.' "

ELVIS: "When there are no exploiters or exploited and only a society of brothers and sisters, then we are going to have the good fish gathered in one basket. I read a speech of Fidel's where he says that in the perfect communist society people will love each other as sometimes they now love each other inside their own families. Then is when we're going to have only *laguneros, guapotes, mojarras, roncadores,* and *róbalos!*"

Several people said that everything was very clear. I said to them that the disciples said the same thing, after hearing this parable. And we went on to the next verse:

Then Jesus asked them:
"Do you understand all this?"
They answered: "Yes, Lord."

I said: "They surely must have understood it in the same revolutionary sense in which you have just understood it. And that means that their 'yes' is the same as 'it's all clear,' which you have said. But that 'yes' also seems to me to be a Yes of commitment. It is accepting Christ's message and being ready to put it into practice. Because the message is not just that the world is going to change but that we have to change right away with a view to that change. That's how Saint Mark sums up the preaching of Jesus in Galilee, on the shores of this lake: 'The times have been fulfilled and the kingdom of God is near. Change your attitude, and believe in the good news.' "

Then he said to them:
"When a master of the law instructs himself
*   about the kingdom of heaven,*
he gets to be like the master of a house,
who from what he has stored away
can bring forth new things and old things."

One of the young people said: "Do you suppose the man takes the old things out of his house to throw away, and the new ones are the ones he'll use? Because the new teachings are the ones that will be followed now, I think. And the old ones are generally not useful."
Another said: "In a house old things are use-

ful just like new things. I think what it means here is that he makes good use of everything."

And DOÑA NATALIA: "You often throw out old things and then you go around looking for them. And this is a man who didn't throw them out but put them away. Later the time comes when there's a need for that old junk that was put away and that didn't look as though it was going to be good for anything."

And another of the young people: "I believe Jesus has given us an example of that, because he uses the Old Testament and he has also given us the new one."

And FELIPE said: "I also think that liberation is old and is new. Because it comes from the time of Moses, and perhaps before then, but it's also a thing of right now. And those two liberations are the old and the new."

ELVIS: "And both are useful to us, right?"

ALEJANDRO: "We used to like certain devotions, the 'Most Blesseds' to the Virgin, the processions, and things like that, and now we don't like them any more. But there are the other things that we *do* use even though they're old. For example, the Feast of Saint Joseph. Now we celebrate it in a different way from what we formerly did. Now the Youth Club organizes it and gives it the meaning of the feast of a worker, of a laborer."

I said, trying to sum up: "It means then that not only is the new good, the old can also be good. There are old things that are thrown out because they are of no use, and there are useful old things that we ought to go on using. So the gospel teaches us to use the old and the new ... "

LAUREANO interrupted me: "And the gospel itself is old but it's being used for today's liberation. Marxism is what's new, and it's also being used together with what's old."

I: "We can also say that love is what is old and new."

And one of the girls: "That's beautiful."

WILLIAM: "It says that when a 'teacher of the law' instructs himself about the kingdom of heaven it's like the man that pulls out old and new pots and pans. The teachers of the law were the scribes, the ones who knew about the Scriptures. Once they got only old things out of them. Now that he already knows about the kingdom he can get old things and new things."

I: "The disciples understood the parables and they said 'Yes' to Christ. Now he tells them that they're going to be like the man who gets old things and new things."

ALEJANDRO: "We have understood it, so now we can get something out of this and give it to others."

10.

Jesus Walks upon the Water

(Matthew 14:22–33)

From the church windows we looked out on a
calm lake. The water at the edges was like a
mirror. From time to time the mirror was
broken by the leap of some huge shad. We had
read a passage where Jesus walked upon the
water. I had said that in Greek "to walk near
the water" may be the same as "to walk upon
the water," and that some people think that
that could have created confusion, and that
the original story might have been only what
is at the end of the narrative: that Jesus had
got into a boat and had calmed the storm. But
we are not going to comment on the event as it
was in reality because we do not know it; we
are going to comment on the narrative as it
has come down to us. And we went on to comment on the verses.

Then Jesus had his disciples enter the boat
to cross the lake before him
and to reach the other shore,
while he said good-bye to the people.
After saying good-bye to them

74

Jesus went up into the mountain
    to pray alone.
When night came Jesus was there alone,
while the boat was in the middle of the lake.
The waves were beating against the boat
because the wind was blowing upon them.

OLIVIA: "The first thing I see here is the
importance of prayer. Jesus said good-bye to
the people so he could pray. And it was so he
could pray that he left his disciples alone, because prayer is important. We see that the
religious practices of the Pharisees, which are
still followed by many Christians, were not
followed by Jesus. But he did pray."

I said: "In order to pray we have to withdraw from other people and even from ourselves and unite with that other person who is
inside us and inside other people and whom we
call God (or Love). And uniting with God is
uniting with all the other people we have become separated from in solitude and in the
night, because God is love."

FELIPE: "Prayer is important for a revolutionary."

I: "At least for a Christian revolutionary. A
non-Christian revolutionary can have other
unions with God by means of sacrifice and love
of others, in a form that is very similar to that
of prayer (and that will often lead one to be
alone as Jesus was there that night)."

ROSITA, the wife of Eduardo, the painter of
primitives, said: "When he was praying, the
disciples were going through a squall, and I

believe he was praying for the disciples. The
same thing has often happened to us here on
the lake when we get in our boats and suddenly there's a squall. But the squall passes
and the lake becomes calm. And I think that he
was praying for us too."

FELIPE: "There are many kinds of squalls.
The gospel makes us see here that we also are
disciples of Jesus who have been sent by him in
a boat to the other shore, so that we'll go without him. Maybe we don't know why he sent us,
and storms might come up. But Jesus has
stayed praying for us there in the mountain,
so nothing will happen to us. Afterwards the
lake will become calm."

In the dawn Jesus approached them,
walking upon the water.
And when the disciples saw him walking
upon the water
they were amazed and they shouted in fear:
"It is a ghost!"
But Jesus spoke to them and said:
"Be brave; it is I;
do not be afraid!"

OSCAR: "It seems that the disciples there
were afraid during the squall, weren't they?
Well, they couldn't imagine that it was Jesus.
Just like us, if we saw a person walking upon
the water, we'd get scared and we might say it
was some idiot who had magic powers. So they
were afraid. Because they were struggling
with an angry lake and they looked at that

man who came walking in the dawn upon the water. They were afraid and they said: 'A ghost!' Any one of us would have felt the same. Then he didn't scold them or anything. He just said: 'Have faith!' He wanted to take away their fear of that storm, which could sink them. And the same thing happens with us, who are often in a boat, as Rosita says, and suddenly a hurricane blows up. And we shouldn't be afraid, because nothing will happen to us. And even if it does, it doesn't matter because if we have faith in him we always live for him. There are not only the squalls of the lake, there are also other storms, for example, like what we're seeing right now, but we mustn't be afraid."

ESPERANZA: "The fact that he walked upon the water means that he can overcome the lake and calm the storm, because he has a mysterious power. So maybe he'll overcome the storm that we're having in Nicaragua."

I: "And in this storm he isn't a ghost, an illusion. He's really himself and so we shouldn't be afraid."

OSCAR: "Then, Ernesto, what we're shown here is that if we have faith in him, we can overcome this squall that we're now struggling with, without any need for him to be present like he was for the disciples, there on the water. We can overcome it if we all get together to struggle against the injustices that the poor are suffering. Because misery gets greater and greater and goods get more and more expensive, and that, I imagine, is a storm for us. If we get together and agree, all of us, we're capable of overcoming that storm."

I: "We might say, then, that that union of all of us is Jesus Christ, who appears walking on the water. The union is Jesus, who approaches us, for he has said that whenever we unite he will be there. And that's why he's not an illusion in our minds or a ghost, because our union is really Jesus in the midst of the hurricane."

A lady said: "I think that's true, because if a community unites (for example, the Nicaraguan people), that union is based on love, and that united people has a great power. We've seen it recently in the hospital strike, and before that we saw it in the construction workers' strike. That shows us the great power that the united people has. And the only thing we lack is more unity, complete unity of everybody to put an end to injustices. Without unity we would be as they were in that storm before Jesus arrived."

MANUEL: "That's what happened with Communism. When it first appeared it frightened people like a ghost, a spook. Now that we've seen it close up we see that it's unity, solidarity among people, the true communion of all with all and also with God. It seems to me that it's like a ghost, and when we come closer we say: 'But it's Christ.' So now there are many peoples that have embarked with that Christ that they used to imagine was a ghost."

I said that Manuel's words reminded me of that famous document by Marx and Engels called the *Communist Manifesto*, which begins

by saying: "A ghost is roaming through
Europe...." And I didn't know whether Manuel was aware of that and was thinking of that
when he spoke of the ghost. (Manuel smiled
and nodded.) I also said that in fact Communism has ceased to be a ghost. It is real, and
we see that there is no reason to be afraid of it
because it means love.

Peter then got out of the boat
and began to walk upon the water
to go to where Jesus was.
But when he noticed the force of the wind
*   he was afraid,*
and as he began to sink he shouted:
"Save me, Lord!"
At once Jesus took him by the hand and said
*   to him:*
"How little faith you have!
Why were you distrustful?"

Another young man said: "You know, Ernesto, I'm beginning to see what Manuel says,
that unity and love are a reality that's
approaching us in the squall. And that ghost
that he mentioned there, well it's like when
there's love, and it's like walking on the water
without being afraid of sinking. And we too
can walk on the water like Peter, who did the
same as Christ. When Christ, that ghost, appeared for the first time to the Communists,
they maybe didn't even realize they were loving. If we succeed in uniting, if we're in a united community, there's nothing to fear. But if
selfishness separates us, we can begin to sink,

like Peter. But loving is like walking on the
water, so it seems to me. It seems that Peter
had faith in him, and he doubted. He had faith
but he also had doubts, and when he saw himself on top of the water maybe he got scared,
because he'd never done that before. He saw
the waves and he wasn't sinking. I'm like that.
I can have great faith in you, and sometimes
you've corrected me because I've done something bad and I say: 'Why does this guy scold
me?' But I say: 'He's right, he knows why he
says that to me, he doesn't want to see me sink,
drown in this lake.' And then I say: 'Man, save
me.' You hold out your hand, you always give
me your hand, and you say to me: 'Don't do it
again,' for example, some mistake I make. You
scold me as Christ scolded Peter."

> *When they got in the boat, the wind died
>   down.*
> *Then those who were in the boat*
> *knelt down before Jesus and said:*
> *"You really are the Son of God."*

The same young man said: "When he got
into the boat the storm was calmed, because
he was love. And the same thing will happen to
us. If we're united in a single person, if we love
each other, we can calm any squall, as I said.
That has happened in Cuba, a country that's
moving the way Jesus Christ wants. Many
people say they don't believe in God. There's
no need to believe in God! The name of God

doesn't save, religion doesn't save, what saves is love."

ALONSO: "When Jesus got in the boat they left their doubt behind. They had believed that he was a ghost, and he was love. When the wind died down and the lake got calm, they had faith in him. They weren't scared any more."

OLIVIA: "When all the people are united by love it must be like Christ getting into that boat. He got in and the water got calm. That's the way it must be for the poor; the squall would calm down and we would recognize that God is there in the midst of us, that there is the Son of God, that all of us united are the Son of God."

OSCAR: "The one who seemed to be a ghost turned out to be love."

And DON JULIO CHAVARRIA, an old man standing in one corner of the church, who rarely spoke: "What's important for us in what has been read, it seems to me, is that these winds blow all the way over here to where we are."

11.

Cure of a Paralytic

(Luke 5:17–26)

We had read the story of the cure of the paralytic according to Luke. Some men carried a sick man on a stretcher to the house where Jesus was but they couldn't get in because the house was filled with people:

> *Then they went up on the roof*
> *and, removing the tiles, they lowered the sick*
>   *man on the stretcher*
> *into the midst of the people,*
> *in front of Jesus.*
> *Jesus saw the faith that they had*
> *and he said to the sick man:*
> *"My friend, your sins are forgiven."*

ALEJANDRO spoke first: "Well, many sicknesses, especially in rich people, are psychological and are due to selfishness. They're selfish and therefore they're nervous and so they get sick. Maybe Christ, by forgiving their sins, by curing them of selfishness, is curing them."

FATHER JULIO, a Spanish Jesuit who had

come to visit us, spoke: "It occurs to me that
here Jesus is making us see that physical illness is not our real illness, which is moral illness. And to cure this illness is really why he's
come. And then he tells him that he forgives
him his sins. You'd wonder what sins he's talking about. It seems to me that the fact that
this person is carried by others on a stretcher
is telling us something more: Sins are an im-
mobility, an incapacity to serve others, and
having to be served by others, or, in effect,
selfishness. That's what he wants to uproot in
this man, to create, so to speak, a new person."

I said that I wanted to take this opportunity
to introduce brother Carlos, a nurse who had
come to help us at Solentiname and who, next
Sunday, was going to vaccinate the children
against polio. And I said also that it's clear in
this gospel that people naturally considered
that physical illnesses were very important.
They brought many sick people to Jesus. They
had changed him into a healer, like Nando, the
healer of Matagalpa. And he really healed.
But that wasn't his mission, as it is the mission
of those devoted to medicine, like our brother
Carlos. Here he wants to make it clear that he
came for another purpose. Perhaps he acted
like this on many other occasions and the gospel speaks of it only once. Maybe at other times
he didn't even cure illnesses, only sins."

ALVARO GUZMAN, a young man who is study-
ing to be a Jesuit and who came with Father
Julio: "It occurs to me (and it might be a little
far-fetched) that the group that carried the

sick man is like the liberation movement that we have in our present system. There are many people who won't let them in. But that doesn't stop them; they come in through the roof. Those comrades acted in a revolutionary way, because when you have something that needs a solution you have to look for all the ways. And when they finally get to Christ, we see that Christ behaves radically toward them. He cures the illness but he's not content with that, in a 'developmentalist' way. He's going to cure the illness radically. And the first thing he does is shape the new person."

FELIPE: "He gave more importance to sin, because sin is injustice to other people. He makes us see that it's the first thing that must be removed."

JULIO MAIRENA: "The gospel says that Jesus was surrounded by Pharisees and teachers of the law. It seems that they are the ones who are always keeping us from getting close to Jesus."

OSCAR: "And it was really selfishness that was surrounding Jesus. Because they were selfish, they wouldn't make way to let the man on the stretcher come in. That's why Jesus wants to make them see that the most important thing is to take away sin, to stop being bastards, it seems to me."

CARLOS, a Spaniard who had been a worker-priest in a mine in Asturias and who had recently married: "What I see in Jesus' miracles is that he wasn't the one that made

the cure; instead it was the individual's faith
that performed the miracle. He usually either
asks about their faith, or their faith is evident.
And I see the same thing in the forgiveness of
sins. It's not a question of getting on your
knees in front of Jesus Christ and saying:
'Forgive me,' if what really forgives us is faith.
Through faith, it seems to me, we're con-
stantly being forgiven for our sins. And I believe that in this struggle for liberation faith is
very important. Christ says that with faith we
can even move mountains."

I said that in fact Christ, when he performs a
miracle, often says: "Your faith has saved
you." And I added what I had read in José
Porfirio Miranda, that in the New Testament
the word "faith" means to believe that Jesus is
the Messiah, and that with him has come the
messianic age, the liberation of all the poor
and the oppressed of the earth. And that's
why, Miranda says, those who believe that
salvation will come only in the next world, that
this world is hopeless, that there will never be
a just society, and that people will always be
selfish, do not have faith according to the New
Testament. But Marxist atheists who do believe in this, even though they don't believe in
God, have that faith that Jesus talks about. I
also said that Jesus' phrase that faith moves
mountains is a reference to Mount Zion, for
the prophets had several times prophesied
that in the messianic age the mountain where
Jerusalem stood was going to change place.

ELVIS: "I see then that what he's saying is that there's going to be a big social change, and that the change will be made by faith."

GLORIA said: "That man had this faith. And this faith had already converted him, that is, it had already made him change his attitude and his mentality, and that's why Jesus tells him that his sins are forgiven."

OSCAR: "Probably not only his sins were forgiven but the sins of his friends, too. Because they all had faith, the whole group, because the gospel says: 'when he saw the faith that they had.' "

OLIVIA: "It seems to me that sickness often comes through sin. For example, in our country, because of the profits they make from medicines, people can't buy them; they can't get cured. Children die for lack of medicines, because medicine is for the people who have money."

I said that there are indeed many illnesses in the country that are illnesses just of the poor and not of the rich, which shows that they are due to the economic system that we have. And it proves that this system is criminal. Infantile paralysis should have been wiped out in this country as it has been in Cuba and in all socialist countries. If many children die here of this illness or are left crippled, it's the fault of the government. I said also that we must be grateful to our comrade nurse Carlos for the vaccinations he's going to give, and that parents must bring their children for the vaccination because otherwise it would not be the government but the parents who would be responsible. In this case polio would be the result of a sin of selfishness in them.

> *Then the teachers of the law*
> *and the Pharisees began to think:*
> *"Who is this man who is offending God with*
> *his words?*
> *No one can forgive sins but God alone."*

FELIPE: "The thing is that the Pharisees didn't believe that Jesus Christ was God."

MANUEL: "That God was in the midst of them."

ALEJANDRO: "They say that only God can forgive sins. Is this right? It seems to me that people can forgive sins. When we forgive one another God forgives us." And he continued, after a pause: "It must be because, since Jesus came, God is in the midst of us."

> *But Jesus knew what they were thinking*
> *and he said to them:*
> *"Why do you think thus?*
> *Which is easier to say:*
> *'Your sins are forgiven'*
> *or 'Rise up and walk'?"*

OSCAR: "Well, man, the way I see it, when Jesus said the sins were forgiven, the ones who were there, the teachers and the Pharisees, were full of doubts, because how could he take away sins? Then he had to show them he could forgive sins and he said to the man: 'Rise up and walk,' so they'd believe. He had to do both, forgive the sins and make him walk. But the hardest thing was what he did first, about the sins."

MIRYAM: "But since they couldn't see that . . . "

I said that's why he had to do things that they could see, and those are the miracles. "Miracle" is a word that means "sign." It had been announced that the Messiah was going to make the blind see, the deaf hear, and the crippled walk, and now he was giving these "signs" or symbolic acts so they would know that the messianic age had arrived.

> *Then he said to the paralyzed man:*
> *"I say to you, rise up,*
> *pick up your stretcher, and go to your house."*
> *At once the paralytic got up in front of them,*
> *took up the stretcher on which he was lying*
> *and went off to his house praising God.*

OSCAR: "The faith that man had was a great faith. But he was helped too by the faith of the others who carried him, who had a faith that came from way inside them. It helps anyone who's a sinner to be united in a single faith with others."

I said: "The proof of that faith is that he went away praising God. Praising God means here that he went away proclaiming that God had already sent the Messiah, the liberator that he had promised."

And CARLOS, the Spaniard: "People alone

cannot free themselves. It occurs to me that each one of us, by ourselves, are like that crippled man, who, no matter how much faith he had, couldn't all by himself get to where Jesus was. It's not enough, it seems to me, for a person to have faith. It's necessary for a group to have faith. So it's only in a community that we can free ourselves."

All were amazed and praised God,
and in much fear they said:
"Today we have seen marvelous things."

FELIPE: "You see, man, they were amazed at what they saw: the paralytic carrying the stretcher. But also they were amazed at the other thing they didn't see, the most marvelous of all: the man with his sins forgiven."

I: "They too went away praising God, that is, proclaiming that Jesus was the Messiah sent by God."

DONALD: "It seems to me that they were very amazed especially because they knew he was the son of a carpenter. If he hadn't been of such a humble origin maybe they wouldn't have been so amazed that God had given such power to a man."

OSCAR: "Ernesto, I ask this question: Why did they have so much fear, then, so much fear that they said: 'Today we have seen marvelous things'? Why did they say that with fear?"

I didn't know what to answer Oscar. I thought that maybe he himself could tell us. I said: "Well, what do you think? Let's see . . . "

OSCAR: "I ask you because I really don't know."

And I: "You don't have the answer? Neither do I. Let's see if anybody has it. If anybody is inspired by the Holy Spirit to answer Oscar ... "

There was a brief silence. Then ALEJANDRO spoke: "I say that maybe it could be the fear that the rich felt because he was always against the capitalists. That is, when they saw he had done something extraordinary, they saw him as a threat to themselves."

And I commented: "It seems to me that Alejandro is quite right. They saw him as an enemy of the system, and they saw that he had the power of God. And they also knew that that power of God was dangerous, for God was in favor of justice, and therefore he was against injustice."

OSCAR: "That's good. It's clear to me now."

12.

Jesus Calls Levi

(Luke 5:27–32)

After this Jesus went out
and he noticed a tax collector named Levi
sitting in the place where taxes were paid,
and he said to him:
"Follow me."
Then Levi got up
and, abandoning everything,
he followed Jesus.

One of the women said: "As I see it this is
very important for us today. We often feel that
humanity is loaded down with sins and that
there's no solution. These tax collectors or
publicans were bad people, detested by decent
people, and rightly so. Nevertheless Jesus
talks with one of them and right away he
changed his attitude and abandoned his dirty
business."

I said that she was quite right, that this
gospel showed us that there is hope for humanity, that people are capable of change.

OSCAR: "Well, I see one thing. That man was
lost, you could say. And just one word was

enough for him to change. I think he knew what he was doing, that he was doing evil. And then Christ noticed him, that he was doing evil and didn't know why. I think he must have been criticized by those who thought of themselves as Christians, right? And they thought there was no salvation for him. Christ knew that he *could* be saved, because Christ was a man who knew what he was doing, and if he talked to him the man would repent. And when Christ said to him: 'Follow me!' it was because Christ was sure that he was going to follow him. And so we, too, who have at some time been bad, and maybe we've been criticized, and we heard the voice, as that man repented, he heard the voice of Christ ... well, I'm all mixed up, I don't know how to go on."

I told Oscar that he wasn't mixed up, that he had explained it very well. He noted one word of the gospel, which said that "Jesus went out and he *noticed* a tax collector." That man was good at heart even though he was doing evil, and that's why Jesus noticed him. If religious people had noticed him it would have been to criticize him (not so much about the money but because he wasn't religious).

REBECA: "He also changed his attitude because he had confidence in Jesus. Just hearing him say 'Follow me,' the man dropped everything he was doing against God and followed him."

FELIPE: "I don't think he knew what he was doing. He was exploiting people, then, out of ignorance—like many people who lead a miserable life devoted only to business because nobody has taught them anything better to do."

Another: "What seems to me important in this gospel is that this man abandoned money for Jesus. His change was a radical change, and he changed just like that."

One of the girls: "Jesus just passed by and said two words to him and he got up and left. People were probably amazed at how he got to the heart of that tax collector."

WILLIAM: "It seems to me that the gospel tells it this way to shorten it, but that it probably didn't happen like that. Jesus first aroused the conscience of the man who was going to follow him. He must have explained to him: 'You are doing wrong, you are swindling the people, you are charging money here just as you please.' And he proposed another plan to him. I think he did the same thing with the fishermen. He would get to the beach, where Saint Peter and his friends were piling up the fish, and he would chat with them: 'And how was your catch?' and so on. He was already their friend, and they knew more or less what he was planning to do. He may have told them: 'Well, one of these days we're going to begin to do some things . . . ' And afterwards he went and told them: 'Well, the time has come, let's go.'

PEDRO: "You also have to keep in mind the moment when Jesus called Levi. Because minutes before he had just performed a miracle, raising up a paralytic. That's why this passage from the gospel begins this way: 'After this Jesus went out. . . .' It was easy for him to say, immediately afterwards to Levi: 'Let's get going.' "

I said that if a revolutionary leader, engaged in a struggle, said to another: "Follow me, come with me," the other would know what that summons meant. So Levi, who was a tax collector of the Roman Empire, knew very well the meaning of "Follow me," said by Jesus, who was a subversive character. The interesting thing is that then "he got up and, abandoning everything, he followed Jesus."

We went on to the other verses. Levi gave a great banquet for Jesus and the Pharisees criticized the disciples:

Why do you eat and drink
with tax collectors and sinners?

OSCAR: "The Pharisees were great Christians but they weren't happy to have another Christian with them."

I told Oscar that the Pharisees didn't call themselves Christians, but they were religious people who believed themselves to be just and did not mix with sinners.

JULIO said: "I have a question, but I don't know if it's a real question. But the Pharisees, it seems to me, were like what we now call Christians, right?"

I: "Like a Christian now, yes. But Christ wanted his community to be made up not of 'just people' (that is, hypocrites), but of repentant sinners."

Another said: "That business of the Pharisees is just like now, man. Because really some of them could be good and those could be Christians as we call them now. And the same with Catholics, too."

Another: "But aren't we the Pharisees of that time right now?"

I said not all of us. That it depended on what we thought about ourselves.

Jesus answered them:
"It is not those who are well and healthy
who need a doctor but the sick.
I have not come to summon the just
but the sinners,
so that they may change their attitude."

OSCAR: "Man, I'm going to talk about myself, then, because I feel I'm a sinner. I'm somebody who's lacking in love. But you know, Ernesto, I'm fully conscious that I'm doing my evil deeds. Maybe some people give me advice, and others criticize me. I see that in spite of the things I do I'm always thinking of God and asking his forgiveness. And I beg him for a repentant heart before death comes to me, because I need resurrection. I get to thinking also that many people were saved even though they were great sinners. Why can't we be saved if we're human beings too?"

I said that there are really no just people,

that we are all sinners, or repentant sinners. When Jesus says he has come not for the just but for the sinners, he may be making a joke, for one of the names that the Pharisees gave themselves was "the just." Jesus has come for all of humanity, which is ill and which must be healed, which is not just but unjust. There are some who believe that people will always be selfish, that there will always be injustice. But Jesus has come so that we sinners (that is, all people) will change our attitudes. And so that all of society will change, as that tax collector changed.

13.

The Question about Fasting

(Luke 5:33–39)

We read this gospel in church. The time for Christmas was approaching (a celebration that we were not going to have because this was the Christmas of the Managua earthquake in 1972).

Then they asked Jesus:
"Why do the followers of John
*   and of the Pharisees*
fast so much and say so many prayers
while your disciples always eat and drink?"

One said: "The Protestants also criticize us in this community because we've had parties and drunk liquor."

Another said: "And there are Catholics, too, who've criticized us because in this church we don't have the prayers and the devotions to the saints that they used to have."

I said that, according to this passage, the disciples of Jesus had no special religious practices but lived like everybody else.

97

Jesus answered them:
"Can you perhaps make the wedding guests
    fast
while the bridegroom is with them?
But the time will come
when the bridegroom will be taken from
    them;
then indeed they will fast."

TOMAS PEÑA: "Well, it seems that there we are told that Jesus' people are very happy because they are with him."

I asked Tomás how he understands the fact that afterwards they will fast when the bridegroom is taken from them, and he said: "Well, sure, when he leaves them. Now he is with them or they are with him. When he leaves them they're going to be sad. Then they're going to pray that he'll be with them again."

OSCAR: "Well, Christ is the bridegroom. When he's taken away, they'll be fasting from Christ. They won't have that food any more, his presence."

I asked if we should now be fasting and praying a lot like the disciples of John and the Pharisees.

FELIPE: "I think if we think about this, that we poor people are so humiliated, we can't be happy. I think we're going to be happy when we're free. Then Jesus Christ *is* going to come to be really with us. So he's alive now, but he really isn't here the way he should be."

OLIVIA: "There are some people who are very happy now, but there are others who are in jail; they and their mothers have no happiness. We must have an equal happiness for everybody."

I said that what they had said was very illuminating to me. I saw that the fast that Jesus announced for his disciples was not exactly like the fast of the disciples of John and the Pharisees. He really likes happiness and parties. He has brought happiness (the good news) to the poor. But we are going to be without him. These are the oppressions and the injustices that we suffer. Only when he comes will we have the true banquet.

TOMAS said: "I believe the followers of Jesus Christ can't be happy as long as they're not free. Of course, we're not unhappy because we're poor, but we're not going to be happy, either."

Somebody else said: "We want happiness for everybody, not just for the rich."

TOMAS: "Of course, we're all looking for happiness, more or less."

WILLIAM: "Yes, but there are advances, progress in that happiness, man. Where there's a community taking shape, where there's a group of united people, there you'll find progress in that happiness. We have to distinguish true happiness from the false happiness of selfish people."

I said we wanted happiness to be spread around and to belong to everyone. Let poor people drink the good wine and the good liquor. Or even better, let them not be poor any more. Let everybody in the country have their

Christmas party. In Cuba, everybody, even the littlest *campesino*, has a Christmas dinner with imported wine and with Spanish Christmas nougat. Everything is rationed a bit, so that there'll be enough for everyone.

WILLIAM: "Which doesn't mean that that happiness won't have problems as well, when it comes. There's got to be problems, people adapting to other people, friction, pesky little things."

But a day will come when all humankind will know perfect love, I said. The prophets have spoken of this as a marriage bond with God, a betrothal. Each time that two people join in marriage they foreshadow that union that all humankind will have with love. And Christ alludes to that wedding when he describes himself as the bridegroom (who for the moment is without the bride). We went on to analyze these other sayings of Jesus:

> *No one cuts a piece from a new garment*
>   *to mend an old garment.*
> *If he does so, he spoils the new garment;*
> *besides, the new piece doesn't go well with the*
>   *old garment.*

FELIPE: "It seems to me, Ernesto, that the teachings of Jesus were new, and so they couldn't be put with the old ones."

I said that in fact they had been asking Jesus about religious practices (fasting and long prayers by the disciples of John and the Pharisees), and he seemed to be telling them now that that was an old religion and that he was bringing something new. They could keep the old garment, if they weren't willing to throw it away just yet, but the new garment was not going to be ruined by using it as a patch on the old garment.

"And what he's bringing, which is completely new, doesn't go very well with the religious practices of Judaism," added WILLIAM.

"In modern language what it means is: I come to bring a revolution. I don't come to mend the old system with patches; I come to revolutionize everything," I said.

FELIPE: "A real revolution, notice. Because all the leaders of that system were against him. Just like nowadays. All the rich people are against the church, or better, against the true Christian religion."

"They are living in the past," I said, "and they don't want anything new, which is brotherhood and love. They are all against change. They are with the old garment."

PEDRO: "A bank is an old garment. You don't cure anything by getting that bank to give a thousand *pesos* to the needy at Christmas time. That's just like sticking on a patch."

Nor does one put new wine into old wineskins;
because, if he does, the new wine bursts the wineskins,
and both the wine and the wineskins are lost.

JULIO: "It seems to me that business of the new wine is the new person. Christians have to be completely new persons in their way of thinking and acting and everything. So they have to be young."

EDUARDO: "We have to begin by gradually making ourselves new then, so we can live in the new society."

WILLIAM: "And it's not enough just to have the new person, as some people say: 'What's important is to change the person, the conversion of the heart.' No, structures need to be changed, too. The new wine has to be in new wineskins. And Christ is also telling us here that the new can't be mixed with the old."

And no one who tastes the old wine
will later want the new,
because he says: "The old is better."

I said that to those who know about wines the mature wine is better than the new wine. But it seems that according to Christ we shouldn't have such tastes. We have to prefer the new wine that he brings above any old wine.

FELIPE: "The old social system, a society of rich and poor, is the old wine. It's better that way for many people, for people who profit from inequality. The new religion is that a few people shouldn't monopolize everything but that everything ought to be shared among everybody. That's the new wine that a lot of people don't like."

Another said: "The old religion suits old people, but not young people."

LAUREANO: "I like the new and I don't like the old."

OLIVIA: "Well, in the old religion they didn't explain the gospels the way they're explained now. The priests began to talk: bla-bla-bla and the gospel . . . It wasn't the gospel, it was a sermon they were giving! I remember a sermon that was given here. It was this, that, and the other, but what did the people want to know about all that. Why, what we wanted was to have it explained and to get something out of it. Now we read the gospels and we're satisfied."

And JULIO said: "It seems to me that we'd already lost our religion. The old-time old folks still had their faith, but it was quite different. And now we have a faith, and we also want happiness, and to live in a new society. Now the gospel has come, and we don't like what we had before."

14.

The Man with the Withered Hand

(Luke 6:6–11)

We read that Jesus was teaching one Sabbath in the synagogue and there was a man there with a withered hand. The teachers of the law and the Pharisees wanted to see if he would cure him on the Sabbath, in order to have something to accuse him of. He said to them:

I am going to ask you a question:
"What is it that one is allowed to do on the day
of rest, good or evil?
To save life or to destroy it?"

I said that among the things one could not do on the Sabbath was to treat sick people, unless they were in danger of death.

Another said: "In order to worship God they failed to help their neighbor. That often happens with religion. Instead of helping others, it helps to continue oppression. We have to oppose that kind of religion as Jesus opposed it."

And another: "They weren't doing anything as far as God was concerned. Because the thing they had least of is what God wanted most of, and that's love."

"There are people who keep religious precepts very well, but when others are suffering hunger, misery, sickness, they don't care. They're just like those Pharisees," said a third.

I referred to some posters on a bulletin board in the church and notices that some young people in Managua had been handing out in the cathedral moments before the earthquake. They spoke of the falsely religious celebration of Christmas while so many poor people in the outlying districts of the city were suffering from hunger. And that night these young people were beginning a three-day fast, in the cathedral, to protest that celebration. And I said that the message of those young people was the same that Jesus gave in the synagogue with regard to the observance of the Sabbath by the Pharisees.

LAUREANO: "There are lots of people who don't want to go to churches like this one of ours, where love is preached, because they don't talk about God in them any more. As if talking about love, about the solidarity of all people, about companionship, wasn't talking about God. And they think that to talk about injustice here is to profane the church."

JULIO: "To have Christ praying in the synagogue seems fine to them. To have him curing a crippled man is a sin. There are a lot of people who still think that way, that the church is for praying but not for curing the ills of society. They don't want us to perform miracles. Because taking care of the needs of others is always performing a miracle for them."

WILLIAM: "Jesus asks them what's permitted on the day of rest, doing good or doing evil. And of course anyone who isn't doing good is already doing evil as a result. Not to cure a man who is ill is to keep him in illness. And so the leaders of the church who say that they don't get mixed up in politics, just by saying this they're getting mixed up in politics, preserving injustice."

I asked why Jesus also talked about saving life or destroying life, when the man wasn't dying but only had a withered hand.

ALEJANDRO said: "There are many ways of destroying life, not just by killing. To keep people in sickness and misery is like destroying their lives, because it's a life that's not a life. Besides, they were already thinking about destroying his life. They were criminals."

> *Then Jesus looked at all those who were surrounding him*
> *and he said to the man:*
> *"Hold out your hand."*
> *The man did so, and his hand was sound.*
> *But the others were very angry,*
> *and they began to wonder what they could do against Jesus.*

REBECA: "Because they were selfish. They had no love for the sick man. They didn't care about anything except keeping the Sabbath. Then when they saw that Jesus performed the miracle, they got very angry, and what they wanted was to kill him. Because that miracle went against their religious practice."

FELIPE: "They were angry because they saw that Jesus had a law different from their law. The same thing happens now with the rich, and with all of us who are selfish: We don't like it when we're told we must help, serve others, share."

TERESITA: "What Jesus was showing them, when he put that man in front of them, is that they had religious traditions that wouldn't allow them to practice love."

I said that among the oldest manuscripts that are preserved from the Gospel according to Luke there is one that has a saying of Jesus not in any other manuscript or recorded by the other evangelists, and for that reason it has been left out of the Gospels. That manuscript says that Jesus saw a man working in the field on the Sabbath and said to him: "My friend, if you know what you are doing, you are blessed; but if you do not know, you are wicked and you are breaking the law." Some think that this may be an authentic saying of Jesus, and I am convinced that it is, because it is very revolutionary. It's hard to think that those words would have occurred to anyone except Jesus himself.

FELIPE: "It's clear. If he had the mentality of the Pharisees but didn't observe the Sabbath, if he thought work was a sin but was doing it anyway, he was doing evil. But if he did the work because he knew that the only precept is the law of love, he was close to the kingdom of heaven. A man who works believing that work

is a sin is doing it out of avarice. The man who
believes that his work is not evil is doing it for
love. He's working for others, not just for himself. He thinks that to plough the field so there
will be bread, even though it's the Sabbath, is
a good thing."

MANUEL: "It means that if a person works
on Sunday, you can say the same thing to him:
If you don't know, if you believe what you've
been taught and you don't conform, you're
evil; but if you know that that precept of not
working on Sunday is nonsense, you're close to
the kingdom of heaven."

I said afterwards that the advances of
medicine were due to Jesus. The first Christians, following the example of his cures, devoted themselves to taking care of the sick.
That wasn't done before. The sick were abandoned to their illness. That Christian concern
for the ill produced the advance of medical
science. But nowadays in capitalist countries
medicine has become very unjust. Its advances are no longer progress for humanity
but a retreat, for most of them are only for the
rich. Often enormous resources are used to
prolong for a little while the life of someone
beyond any hope of recovery, while countless
children are dying for lack of the most elemen-
tary medical services. The same thing can be
said about this classist medicine that was said
by Jesus: That not to do good is to do evil. That
not to save a life is to destroy it.

WILLIAM: "The truth is that in today's world
there are two kinds of people: Some are on the
side of life and others are on the side of death."

15.

The Other Cheek

(Luke 6:27–31)

But to you who hear me I say:
"Love your enemies,
do good to those who hate you,
bless those who curse you,
pray for those who insult you."

There was a long silence. Nobody spoke. We heard only the hubbub of some children playing in the church, and outside the murmur of the lake. I asked if anyone had any comments to make. Everyone kept silent.

"What do you say, Laureano? Don't you want to speak?"

He smiled and said: "No, I don't want to speak; that nonsense is very confusing. That's crazy."

OLIVIA: "That's a very difficult thing, but we have to do it, because the gospel orders us to do it. The words are very clear."

I asked if they thought this was practiced much here in Solentiname. And some answered Yes and others No.

ANDREA, Oscar's wife, said: "Nonsense! We

answer evil with evil. When they insult us, we insult back."

Another said: "I believe this *is* practiced quite a lot in this group."

LAUREANO: "It's true that we don't usually insult each other."

REBECA: "I understand that God wants us all to love each other, not to have enemies, because he has come to give us love here on earth. He hasn't come to give us hatred. Then what he wants is for all of us to love each other and not to have enemies. For all of us to treat each other with love, because he ordered it and that's how it's written."

I said: "Rebeca has told us one thing very clearly: The kingdom of God is love, and therefore we cannot have hatred in that kingdom. And therefore we are commanded to love our enemies. Is that clear enough?"

WILLIAM asked: "Even class enemies?"

I said: "In the class struggle we are struggling to put an end to the division into classes. As long as we are divided into classes, with opposed interests, we have to have class enemies. But if we struggle to unite with them and to form all together a humanity united in classless society, then we are struggling for love and not for hatred. Marxists sometimes talk about hatred. And Che has a phrase or two in which he says that the revolutionary must hate. But I think that is just a way of talking, a little like what Jesus says: 'He who does not hate his father and his mother is not worthy of me.' We Christians have always said: 'We must hate sin and love the sinner.' I have the impression that Che never fought because of hatred of other people but because of hatred of injustice. I was very pleased by a phrase that I heard from a Marxist priest in Chile, Father Arroyo, on one occasion when we had a small Eucharist in his home. A priest was defending revolutionary hatred and he said to him: 'Only love is revolutionary, hatred is always reactionary.' "

OLIVIA: "What Rebeca said was very well put: God is love and he has come to give us love, and we must have love and give each other love. But love is not expressed by repeating that little word 'love.' Love is expressed simply by loving each other. If someone doesn't love you and you can help him out in some way, you can put an end to that hatred. Love destroys hatred. This commandment I believe is for unity."

FELIPE: "And so in the community there would be no enemies. This is also a practical teaching, then, for the community."

MANUEL: "But we have class enemies. And how are we going to manage to struggle against the enemy if we have to love him? How are we going to defend ourselves?"

MARCELINO, slowly: "If we hate, we are no longer struggling against the enemy ... We are the enemy, because we are evil ... He says we must love the enemy, but he doesn't say we can't fight them ... The question is how are we going to fight them. If they hate, the weapon against them is love. The difference between us and the enemy is that we fight them without wanting to oppress them, only to liberate them. They do hate us. But we are no longer the opposite of them if we answer hatred with hatred . . . I say that it is with love that we can defend ourselves."

If someone strikes you on one cheek,
offer him also the other cheek.
And if someone takes your coat from you,
let him have your shirt also.

JULIO RAMON, incredulous: "Does this mean that the poor person must suffer and let people take his things away from him?"

LAUREANO: "It seems to me that this applies to the rich: They should let people take their things from them. He talks about a coat, right? And poor people are always in shirtsleeves [laughter]. So when the revolution comes and their farms are taken away, their factories, their extra houses, they shouldn't put up any resistance. And if they lose one piece of property, let them offer up the other piece."

FELIPE: "Let them give it up freely and give more than is asked of them. This is for the haves. What can the poor give, if they don't have anything? The Christian should be detached from everything, not wanting to defend property with force."

MANUEL: "Then what it says about the other cheek is only for the rich, and the poor should never turn the other cheek?"

I said: "This is also a precept for the poor,

and it is very revolutionary. I mean that we
must pass over our own personalities, put
aside all personal pride and all individualism,
fight not for our own interests but for those of
other people. This doesn't mean not to fight. It
means not to fight for yourself but for others.
And Christ says to turn the other cheek, but
it's *your* other cheek, not the other cheek of
other people. Christians who don't fight for
the revolution aren't turning either one of
their two cheeks. They're turning the cheeks
of undernourished children, of the hopelessly
ill, of abandoned widows, of workers robbed of
their work."

WILLIAM: "And I believe that in the revolutionary struggle, turning the other cheek,
your own other cheek, is also a very effective
weapon. The man who gives the punch feels
worse than the man who takes the punch. The
work stoppage, the peaceful demonstration in
front of guards armed with machine guns, the
hunger strike, the takeover of factories or
churches or universities: all these are turning
the other cheek. And I remember what Gigi,
our Peruvian friend, was telling us about what
the students in Lima had done during the
Belaúnde regime. When a guard was beating a
student the rest of the students would speak to
the guard with love and so would disarm him.
And if the guard went on beating, they would
say: 'Hit him harder, if it makes you feel good,
hit him harder, don't stop, hit him.' It's a way
of appealing to the good that's in the hearts of
the most evil of people. And something like

this happened here with that guard who was
bothering us so much because of what we were
saying in these meetings and he kept on saying that he was going to screw us because we
were Communists. The boys and girls of the
Youth Club went and talked with him in a
friendly way. They treated him with love, and
he changed. Not right away. At first he denounced them to the commanding officer at
San Carlos, saying that a group of young people had gone to his house to attack him. And he
went on saying bad things about all of us. The
group went back again. They told him he was
poor like them, one of the exploited. And he
admitted that he was, that he was very badly
paid. Now, even though he's not in that post,
now he's even our friend. And it was clear that
at heart he was not an evil person. He was a
guy who thought he had to be evil because he
was a guard. And when he saw some friendly
human beings, who didn't answer him with
hatred, he changed, and his bad will toward us
disappeared. This too is blessing those who
curse us, doing good to those who hate us.
There are some other examples of this. When
Batista's army would capture guerrilla fighters, they murdered them at once; when the
guerrilla fighters took wounded prisoners,
they took care of them and then set them free.
Che tells how once when Fidel freed some
wounded prisoners, he gave them what little
medicine was left. And Che protested to Fidel
because their troops were left without any
medicine. But Che behaved just the same in

Bolivia. Inti Peredo, who fought with him, tells how he treated the enemy without any ill feeling and took care of their wounds. General Torres, who was just overthrown in Bolivia, earlier fought against Che's guerrilla fighters and was captured by them. He told how he became a leftist because of the good treatment that Che had given him and because of the discussions they had had. This also is offering the other cheek to the armed enemy. But there is a saying of Martí's that Che repeated a lot: that we ought to feel any blow to anyone anywhere in the world as if it had been on our own cheek."

DONALD: "It's obvious that the greatest example of that was given by Jesus Christ himself, who forbade his disciples to use arms to save him and who died praying for his enemies."

ALEJANDRO: "A clarification: It's a different thing to let yourself be beaten because you're weak or a coward. You do it because you're brave. And sometimes maybe you won't turn the other cheek but will react differently. When Jesus was beaten in the house of Caiaphas, he protested against the man who struck him, and he reasoned with him. Maybe by this he was trying to show us what he meant by 'turning the other cheek.'"

I said: "These words of Christ can be understood in a reactionary way (and they have been so understood many times) or in a revolutionary way, as we are understanding them now. And I believe that the only correct way of understanding them is the revolutionary way."

TOÑITO (a student who is going to be a Jesuit): "But we must also remember what it says at the beginning: 'But to you who hear me I say ... ' He's talking to the poor. They must love each other. If somebody takes something away from you, maybe they need it more than you do, and then you shouldn't ask to have it back."

RAMON: "Then are we defending injustice? The person who takes from us what we maybe need? The poor have to defend what little they have because what they have isn't enough for them. Can the rich take things away from the poor?"

REBECA: "Jesus is talking inside the justice area. Everything is justice there, because the gospel has no injustice. Everything will have to be done with justice, without exploiting anybody. We have to give ourselves to each other, but all inside the justice area, with no exploitation, no selfishness among us. That's the way it seems to me."

ADANCITO, softly: "If we all ought to give things to each other, how much more should the rich hand over what doesn't belong to them, and how much more reason there is to keep the rich from taking things from the poor."

GLORIA, Olivia's pretty young daughter: "Well, the only thing to do is to struggle so we'll all live equal, nobody will exploit us, nobody will oppress us, nobody will be rich, and nobody will be poor."

Give to anyone what he asks of you;
and he who takes from you what is yours,
do not ask him to give it back.

"It's the same thing in different words," said somebody.

"But stronger," added somebody else.

TOÑITO: "I believe we shouldn't understand this just passively: that when somebody takes something from us that they need, we should give it to them. We're also shown that when we don't have what we need we ought to take it. If somebody has more things than they need and somebody else needs them, they are obliged to give them up. The gospel is saying it here. And therefore we're obliged to take them away, I believe."

JULIO (after we have all been silent): "I think this is clear. Why should they take things away from the poor if we don't have anything? The gospel must be talking here of taking things away from the rich, who are the ones that have things."

I said that we see clearly that here it says that those who have must give, and that they mustn't try to keep things but share them with others. And so we'll have that society that Gloria talks about, in which we're all equal.

DON VENTURA: "And if somebody steals? Should stealing be permitted also?"

TERESITA: "If somebody steals, you have to give to that one, too. Maybe not your shirt, but certainly some instruction. He did what he did through ignorance. He has to be taught that he shouldn't do it."

Do unto others
as you wish them to do unto you.

JULIO: "Just as the rich want us to work for them, so also they should work for us."

I said that this system is called socialism. Everyone works for everyone.

FELIPE: "To want for everyone what we want for ourselves means that we're all going to be equal."

I said that here Christ is really planning a new society for us. I asked Laureano: "Now do you agree?"

He smiled. He blushed a little. I asked him again: "Is it clearer now?"

He nodded. And he said: "I was very confused before."

16.

Do Not Judge Others

(Luke 6:37–42)

Do not judge others,
and God will not judge you.
Do not condemn others,
and God will not condemn you.

OLIVIA: "I think 'judge' means to think evil about somebody. I'm missing a ring and I think that what's-her-name stole it. And maybe she didn't. I judged her unfairly."

Somebody else said: "But you can suspect somebody if she is suspicious . . . "

And another: "But you can't be certain if it's not clear to you."

TOMAS PEÑA: "That means that you ought to talk about what you see and not talk about what you don't see."

OLIVIA: "Well, if we talk when we see, we're not judging."

TOMAS again: "In other words, talking about what you don't know about."

ALEJANDRO: "It seems to me that the word 'judge' means to make a judgment on a person.

The other thing would be false evidence, or slander."

FELIPE, Tomás's son: "To judge here, it seems to me, means to condemn. Because it says in the same verse: 'Do not condemn others.' "

FELIX: "And how many times we condemn others unjustly. The jails are full of innocent people, because a person can be jailed for a simple suspicion: I mean if he's poor and has nobody to defend him."

JOSE ARANA: "And how often the innocent are in jail and the criminals go free."

Forgive, and God will forgive you.

Somebody asked: "And how can you do this in today's society, forgive crimes?"

GIGI, our Peruvian friend, answered: "This can't be applied to today's society, which is unjust. But a Christian society, or a revolutionary society, which is the same thing, can and must reach the point of having no repression, no jails, no police."

TERESITA: "But can't a community judge, a community like ours?"

MARIITA: "It seems to me that a just community, that is, a community like this one, can judge."

WILLIAM: "This passage refers to the judges (in the current system), the police, the guards, that is, all those who do the repressing. But it also applies to us. We have to treat each other with forgiveness and not with harshness, and nobody should act as a judge or a policeman or a guard toward his brother. Nobody should control anybody, because we're all equal and nobody is better than anybody else."

DONALD, Alejandro's brother: "We must forgive each other's offenses and go on treating each other always like brothers. Like brothers who get along well and not like brothers who get along badly."

"And as for forgiveness in this society," said someone else, "the truth is that the rich are always absolved and the crimes of the poor are punished very harshly. There is no forgiveness for them if they are poor."

I said that a boy had been here who was a delinquent, one of those who broke into homes. He had reformed and he told us that they would arrest the thieves in Managua and a week later they would free them if they promised to pay a thousand *pesos* to the police and the lawyer. And then the thief had to break into another house to get the money; soon afterward he would be arrested, even though he hadn't done anything, and once again he would have to steal to pay the thousand *pesos*. And so he could never reform (although some of them wanted to). This boy hadn't stolen a thing for two years but they kept arresting him. Finally, although he was no longer a thief but an honest Christian, he had to steal a wallet from a man to be able to pay his fare to somewhere else.

GIGI said: "But in Cuba and in China they don't usually arrest delinquents. They put

them on farms where they are out in the open
air working on something productive and getting trained and they have sports and get
political education and they can go to visit
their families on weekends. So they get rehabilitated, not punished by society but forgiven by society. And it seems to me that
that's what the gospel is telling us here, that
there shouldn't be jails or punishments, and
that the only law of society should be the law of
love."

> *Give to others, and God will give to you.*
> *He will put into your purse a full measure,*
> *packed down, shaken down, and stuffed.*
> *Because with the measure with which you*
>   *measure,*
> *you will be measured.*

I said that the measure was a measure of
grain. Jesus was talking to them in *campesino*
language, as we might say a "bushel."

LAUREANO: "This must apply to those who
have something to give. And those who have
something to give are the ones who don't give.
We don't have anything to give; the poor don't
have to give anything."

OLIVIA: "Nevertheless the poor give a tiny
bit of what they have. There's scarcely a poor
person who won't give to another brother, to
another neighbor. If he has a pound of salt, he
shares it with his friend who asks for some.
And he never lets him go away without what
he needs."

I said: "There's one application for the rich,

the one that Laureano has made, and there's another application for the poor, the one that Olivia has made. There are different social classes, and the gospel doesn't apply equally to all the classes. The rich ought to give, as Laureano has said, until we are all equal and there are no classes and we have a society in which everything is shared just as the poor share that pound of salt that Olivia speaks of. There is a saying of Jesus which is not in the Gospels but which we know through Saint Paul, who must have heard it from someone who had heard Jesus say it: 'It is better to give than to receive.' But it is also good to know how to receive. There are some who know how to give but not to receive. And there are some who don't know how to give or to receive. They only know how to buy and sell."

GIGI: "But when we all give and receive, as Christ says, what we'll share with the generosity of the pound of salt will no longer be a pound of salt but a great abundance and wealth for everyone."

MARCELINO: "It's not only money that you can give: also knowledge, teaching people to read. Or you can give time, working for the Cooperative, for community causes."

COSME: "Another thing you can give is good advice."

JULIO: "And that's something that poor people can really give to rich people."

"What advice?" someone asked. And JULIO answered: "To give to the poor. To stop being rich."

GIGI: "And then we'll have a different society, without rich people, when everyone will give their work and their time, not to pile up things for themselves but for all of society."

"First they have to begin to give back what doesn't belong to them," said somebody.

And REBECA: "But the rich, if they're going to understand these things, have to read the Scriptures. Because the rich who don't even read the Scriptures don't understand anything. They're deceived by their selfishness. God knows the rich, and he said it would be hard for them to be saved, unless they study the Scriptures."

I said that there have been some rich people who have really studied the Scriptures. Then money no longer interested them and they devoted themselves to serving others. That had been the case with many saints, and also with many revolutionaries. And nowadays among middle-class families there are young people who have no interest in money, because they are Christians or revolutionaries, or because they are at the same time Christians and revolutionaries."

"Those have already stopped being rich," said someone.

OLIVIA: "Rebeca said that the rich should know the Scriptures, but the truth is that they know them, but they don't pay any attention to what they say. They're more interested in money than in salvation, it seems to me."

REBECA: "But if they understood the Scriptures, these Gospels, they would change."

COSME: "There are people who don't come close to believing in anything!"

TOMAS PEÑA: "They don't like to hear these things. If they hear them at Mass, they probably leave and go to another Mass."

JULIO: "They know, man! What happens is that they don't do what they know they should. There are others who don't read the gospel but they practice everything it says and they stand for love and everybody being equal."

TOMAS: "I imagine some would rather go on some spree, to one of their great parties, than go to Mass. Because they probably say: 'Everyone there will be taking shots at me. Because there's a lot of poor people there and they're going to be fighting with me.' "

OSCAR: "There are a lot of people who don't have any religion and they say their God is money."

I said: "There are others who want to be both Christians and rich. Even Christians and millionaires. And they think they can do this if they give to charity."

OLIVIA: "It seems to me that this business of our giving to others so that God will give to us, or that God will give to us as we give to others, is the same as saying we must do to others as we want them to do to us. Because the truth is that God does to us as we do to others."

MANUEL: "It seems to me that the business about filling the purse with a full measure is that God always gives more to those who give.

He increases what they have. I mean he makes them more generous, he makes them better hearted, he gives them more love. And also in the resurrection he can give them an even better prize, now that they're free."

GIGI: "Giving doesn't make you poor is what the Gospel says here; giving makes you rich. Rich in love, as Manuel has said, but also in material things. I mean that in an economy based on giving and not taking away there's much greater abundance of material goods than in an economy of avarice and selfishness."

WILLIAM: "But the main prize, it seems to me (the filled purse, the full measure), is sharing it all with others. It's love."

OSCAR: "But look, William: with the same measure that you give with, you receive. Because if you are hardened toward another person, your heart hardens. If you see another as evil, and he's not evil, it means that you're evil. And to the extent that you see someone as evil when he isn't, to that extent you're evil. So judging another person as evil makes me evil. Condemning another condemns me."

Can a blind man perhaps act as a guide for
another blind man?
Won't they both fall into some hole?

OLIVIA: "That's the priests who don't know about this. They read the gospel a lot and they don't know that it's against the rich. And they get you all confused. I remember the priests

used to preach to us that the Protestants were
blind guides. But they themselves were on the
side of the rich and the powerful. They were
really the blind guides. Catholics or Protestants, blind guides are the ones who read the
gospel that says, 'Woe to you rich!' and they're
so comfortable they don't see it. They
preached a lot of things, but they didn't preach
love, and they didn't practice love. And we
were blind in that same chain, and we didn't
show any love for others either."

MANUEL: "Blind Christians led by other
blind Christians. The wrong leading the
wrong."

MARIITA: "I think there are parts of the gospel that they don't read. They don't know
about this."

GIGI: "They do read it but they don't understand it. They explain it to themselves some
other way."

OSCAR: "I don't think they read it. If they did
they'd understand it as it is, because it's very
clear. The rich know more than the poor because they've studied a lot, yet we poor people
understand this. Why don't they understand it
if we understand it?"

GIGI: "The rich have studied more than the
poor, as Oscar says, but they don't know more
than the poor. They don't know more than you
do, and the proof is that all this is very clear to
you but they don't understand it."

WILLIAM: "It says 'fall into the hole.' The
hole is the society of injustice and exploitation
into which we've fallen. Because the guides

were blind. And all the people have been blind with them. This is alienation. Until the time comes when the people open their eyes, and this is conscientization."

No disciple is more than his teacher,
although when he ends his studies
he will become like his teacher.

"The teacher is Jesus Christ," said GLORIA.

REBECA: "Those who live in great luxury, it seems to me, whether bishops, priests, or any other disciples of Christ, want to be more than their teacher, because their teacher was poor."

MARIITA: "At the Last Supper he began to serve them with an apron on to make them see that he was their servant. This way he tried to teach them that nobody should be the master of anybody else, but that we must all be servants of each other. That was his teaching."

WILLIAM: "He was a carpenter like José Arana, and a man of the people. And anyone who wants to be above the people wants to be more than Jesus."

OSCAR: "The studies will end in glory, in the other life. And then the disciples will be glorious like Christ, but only if they were equal to him in this life."

JULIO, his brother: "It seems to me that studies are the awareness that we develop about equality, the conscientization, feeling that we're all equal. And at the end of the studies will come the glory, when all of us are going to be really equal."

"Christ is equal to all of us, and there won't be teachers anymore because we'll all be equal to one another and also equal to Christ," I said.

> *How can you see the mote in your*
>   *brother's eye*
> *and not see the beam that is in your own eye?*
> *How can you say to your brother:*
> *"Brother, let me remove the mote that is in*
>   *your eye?"*
> *Hypocrite! First take out the beam from*
>   *your eye*
> *and you will thus be able to see well*
> *to take out the mote from your brother's eye.*

DONALD: "You can always see clearly the evil in others and not the evil in yourself. But this is not seeing clearly. Because if you have a beam in your eye you're not seeing anything."

OSCAR: You see the other person's error and not your own (or *my* own, I mean; why should I say 'you'?). And that's an error that I commit. Maybe bigger than the error that I'm looking at. It's the same as I was saying before, about judging: the way I judge I'm judged. Because if I judge bad I make myself evil. Noticing somebody else's speck is judging him, is seeing him evil, and that makes me worse. Because I don't do it to reform him but because I think I'm better, and therefore I'm worse. I'm a blind man who wants to guide others when I have a beam in my eye and how am I going to remove a speck when I can't see ... Well, I'm all mixed up, let somebody else talk."

MANUEL: "The hypocrites are the Pharisees,

right? And the Pharisees were the guides of the people, right? Then the blind guides are the hypocrites who want to reform others without reforming themselves. The disciples of Jesus may be Pharisees, and the revolutionaries may be Pharisees, if they don't criticize themselves."

JULIO: "I've been talking against the rich, but I see that what's here can be applied to the poor as well: not to blame everything on the rich, because maybe the poor are just alike, except that they don't do some things because they can't. So first we ought to change ourselves so that later we can demand that the rich change themselves."

WILLIAM: "This is an important call for self-criticism. Also for criticism, because you can remove the mote from your brother if your eye is clean. Here in the Youth Club there's a lot of criticism and self-criticism. After they've had a party, for instance, they examine what things were bad and what were good, what was positive and what was negative."

"Is that all?"

"We've seen it all clearly," said MILAGROS.

When the comments were over I informed them that we had learned that one of the people present in the church (Mario, the schoolteacher) was a spy. We had also learned that his real name wasn't Mario and that he wasn't a teacher but a captain in the army. He changed color, protested with a lot of false starts that he was not a spy but a revolutionary. I insisted that we had proof. But that we were not judging him or condemning him.

FELIX said: "What does it matter if he's in the secret police, if that's how he earns his living? As long as he doesn't lie."

MARIITA: "As long as he just says what he sees and hears. Because this is the gospel, and we say it publicly."

17.

The Tree Is Known by Its Fruits— And the Two Foundations

(Luke 6:43–49)

> *There is no good tree that can produce bad*
> *   fruit;*
> *Nor is there a bad tree that can produce good*
> *   fruit.*
> *For each tree is known by its fruits:*
> *you do not harvest figs from thorn trees,*
> *nor do you pick grapes from bramble bushes.*

FELIPE: "Jesus says that people are like trees. Because people, like the trees, produce fruit. But the people who are good can't produce evil, and the people who are evil can't produce good. There is one way of knowing ourselves and it's by what we do. We may think we're good, but if we do evil we're evil. And people can say we're evil, but if we do good things we're good."

My brother FERNANDO, who is a Jesuit and visiting with us now: "Which means that being and doing are the same thing and can't be separated. Or rather, what people are is known by what they do. And doing, it seems to

132

me, is the same as the way you behave toward others. Depending on our relations with others, we are bourgeois or revolutionaries."

REBECA: "People produce good fruits who do the will of God, which is love. And people who act in accordance with love can't produce bad fruit. And people who don't act the way God wants them to are people who act out of selfishness, and they can't produce good fruit."

MARCELINO, Rebeca's husband: "We know plants. City people don't know them and often they can't tell a *zapote* from a *sonzapote*. And I think we have to sort out people like we sort out trees. According to the gospel there are two classes of people: good and evil. That's the same as saying: the just and the unjust, the exploited and the exploiters. And we *campesinos* have to be clear about which is which."

DONALD: "As I understand it, trees are only good or only bad. But it seems to me there are people who are half and half, who sometimes do good and sometimes do evil."

ADAN: "Selfish people never do good. And we see this in the rich. They don't have any good fruit. They always act according to their interests, and their interests are against us."

FELIPE: "Evil people, even though they act good, they do it bad, because what they do very well is doing evil. Or they do good to hide the evil, and we can't say that's good."

FELIX: "Evil people can do good things, too: for instance, a rich person who gives to charity."

JULIO: "If evil people do good deeds it's for their own interests. We think they're doing us good. They do good to get a double profit."

EDUARDO, the painter: "Maybe their gift to charity is money they took from somebody else."

REBECA, emphatically: "But the bad tree never gives good fruit. All year long it gives the same bad fruit. And if it's a good tree, all year long it gives good fruit."

ALEJO: "I understand this about trees. Trees can never change. The *jobo* will never give *jocotes*. But can't the evil person ever get to be good?"

I said that people can change and that that's what the gospel talks most about: a change of attitude. In this we are different from trees. But we also see that, according to the gospel, while we are good all our fruits will be good and while we are evil they will all be evil.

FERNANDO: "You could also say that in a good system everything is good and that in a bad system everything is bad. Capitalism can't produce good fruit because it's based on selfishness; it produces only exploitation. Some say that it's more important to change people than to change the system, but the truth is that there are many people who are individually good in a bad system and the system forces them to be evil. In a system of exploiters and exploited, many who don't want to be exploited are obliged to be exploiters. I think people are as important as the system, and both must change at the same time. The good system produces a new person, but that

new society or kingdom of heaven is not going
to drop down from heaven. It's going to rise up
out of our own depths, like a good fruit."

I said that Silverio only last Tuesday had
gone to the San Carlos clinic because he had an
earache, and at the Clinic they sold him a
medicine (which they should sell at cost there)
at a higher price than in the drugstore. A mer-
chant commented that they did that only to
the poor because they had no way to defend
themselves, and that wealthy people got
medicines cheap or for nothing. And I said
that here we saw that in an evil system like
ours even the good things (like clinics, hospitals, doctors, nurses, etc.) were all evil.

OLIVIA: "I like it that we're applying this
overall, to society as a whole, about the tree
and its fruits, and not in detail, to individual
cases. Because the fruits of this society are
very evil. Many, many people come down from
the hills in poor health and they go back the
way they came because they don't get cured in
the clinic or the hospital, and those people
have to go back home to die. And this isn't just
in San Carlos; it's in the whole republic. Even
if you beg him the doctor won't knock anything
off the price of the medicine. But the rich who
can afford to buy it get it free. Most poor people
when they get sick have to die or stay sick.
That's why we're all sick all the time."

WILLIAM: "And it seems to me that what
Jesus is also telling us with this example about
the laws of nature is that good and evil in
people also obey the natural laws of history,
which are also called the laws of historical ma-

terialism. The relationships of production in a given society will determine the spiritual fruits that are produced. For a system of exploitation to produce love among people is as unnatural as it is for thorn trees to produce figs."

The good man says good things
because good is in his heart;
and the evil man says evil things
because evil is in his heart.
For with his mouth he says what his heart is
*   filled with.*

I said that it seemed like Jesus was talking about deeds (fruits) and now we see that he is referring to words. Can it be that he has changed the subject?

FELIPE: "Words are a kind of deed."

I asked if evil people couldn't say good things (politicians?), and an old man, DON JULIO CHAVARRIA, answered me: "Here he means good things that agree with the deeds. It's not a question of saying 'I'm good, I'm good,' and praising myself. Lies, falsehoods are not good. If a person is false, his words are lies because falsehood is in his heart, and the heart is all of him. If I have an evil heart, I have to say evil things."

"Those evil things that evil people say and that come out of their hearts," I said, "are what exploitation is, like the words with which they sold Silverio that medicine, like all the words of business and the banks and the newspapers and the capitalist radios, and like the laws, the court sentences, and the orders to jail and to shoot."

COSME the boatman asked: "And how about those people that all they do is repeat these Scripture words but don't live them?"

"They are talked about right here in this gospel," said GLORIA, and she read the following verse:

Why do you call me, "Lord, Lord,"
and you don't do what I tell you?

ALEJANDRO said: "Those are the Christians that we've had for so long, the Christians that are religious but don't live the gospel."

FERNANDO: "It spoke earlier of the good words that spring from the good heart. These words don't spring from the heart, because they're not true, or better, they spring from an evil heart. It spoke earlier about the true words that are like good fruits, that are words that are translated into action. And now it wants to distinguish them from those other words, like the 'Lord, Lord,' which are straight formula and religious ritualism. In another passage Jesus has said that it won't be the ones that say, 'Lord, Lord,' who will enter the kingdom of heaven; it'll be the ones that do the will of the Father. That means the ones who will be saved aren't necessarily the religious ones but the ones who fulfill that will, which is love."

FELIPE: "Talking without doing anything is no good for anything."

I said: "The word is heard in order to carry it

out. 'Do for others what you want them to do for you,' according to Jesus, is the summary of the word of God (the Law and the Prophets). And saying, 'Lord, Lord,' seems to be praying, and also confessing that Jesus is God, for in Greek the word 'Lord' *(Kyrie)* also means God, and the first recognition that was made of the divinity of Christ, after his resurrection, was to apply to him the word *Kyrie* (Lord). But according to Jesus, neither invoking him nor believing in his divinity ('believing in Christ,' as we say) brings us salvation, but instead it's doing what he says. And this 'Lord, Lord,' reminds us also of those virgins who got left out of the wedding feast and according to the gospel in Greek, what they were crying was *Kyrie! Kyrie!*"

LAUREANO: "Really to believe in Christ is not to believe he's God but to do what he says, whether we believe or don't believe he's God."

*The man who comes to me and listens to me
and does what I say,
I will show you what he is like:
He is like a man who built a house,
but first he dug very deep
and laid the foundation upon the rock. . . .
But the one who listens to me
and does not do what I say
is like a man who built his house on the
    ground, without a foundation;
and when the river rose
and beat against it,
it collapsed and great was the ruin of that
    house.*

FERNANDO: "Jesus divides people into two classes, not into believers and atheists, but into those who act and those who don't act. We could also say: those who love and those who don't love. And I remember now what the Apostle Saint James says: We must be 'doers of the word,' because the one who only listens to the word 'is deceiving himself.' Carrying out the word, according to Jesus, is building upon rock. In the Old Testament God was called 'Rock,' because rock is strong and with it walls and fortresses are built. In the New Testament Jesus is also called 'Rock,' and here he is telling us what that rock really is. The rock is love."

OSCAR: "A house is to live in together, united, the whole family (this occurs to me now that I'm building my farmhouse). But false religion can't be that house we all live in, because it has false foundations, it's doomed to disappear; it's not going to last long."

MIGUEL: "I think it's already falling down . . . "

LAUREANO: "The shifting earth that house was built on is like our class society."

ALEJANDRO: "Doctrine alone, the knowledge of Jesus' words, the Bible itself: These are things that have no value by themselves. Building just on that is building on the surface. You have to build on actions, on love put into practice: the praxis of love."

WILLIAM: "And I think it can also be interpreted this way: that we can't build a just social system based only on ideas or doctrines (as we Christians have often believed). We have to base it on material realities, what Marxists call the infrastructure, which is the way we produce bread, clothes, houses. We first have to create a fair infrastructure, brotherly economic relations among people, so that the superstructure (things like ideas, philosophy, morals) will also be good. Otherwise the whole structure will go down the drain, which is what will happen with today's society. The river that overflowed was the current of history, which is also called the revolution. The man who built that house without a foundation also failed to notice that he was near a river."

FERNANDO: "And what he says at the end, that the ruin was very great, reminds me of the experience we've just gone through in the great Managua earthquake. Then we saw not just that there were many badly built houses but that the whole structure of society was badly built, based only on profit and selfishness, and that's why the ruin was so great. Even the foundations of the houses were weak because the whole of society was based on exploitation. And there were people who owned forty, fifty, eighty houses, and in twenty seconds they lost them. The moral ruin of those people was also very great, because they had based their happiness on those riches. The same thing will happen when the revolution comes, with all those who have built their lives on false bases."

FELIPE: "And at the hour of the earthquake maybe those people were saying: 'Lord, Lord!' "

I said that a friend told me that at the time of the earthquake many people who had never prayed went down on their knees to pray in the streets, while the authentic Christians didn't pray: They were busy helping others. I asked if anyone had any other comment to make. After a silence, someone answered: "Nobody."

18.

Jesus Sends Forth the Twelve

(Luke 9:1–6)

We were in the meeting hut. We had had a simple meal of rice and beans.

> *Jesus called together his twelve disciples*
> *and gave them power and authority*
> *to cast out all kinds of evil spirits*
> *and to cure sicknesses.*
> *He ordered them to announce the kingdom of*
>   *God*
> *and to cure the sick.*

REBECA said: "It seems to me that it's to show forth love. Because they are going to announce the kingdom of God and the kingdom of God is love. And he gives them those powers so that people will understand, because sometimes people don't understand what the kingdom of God is. Many people think the kingdom of God is heaven, after death, but what they were going to announce was the kingdom of love among people. They had to make people know what love is. When they cured the sick and cast the evil spirits out of people they were beginning to bring about that kingdom on earth."

Someone else said: "They're announcing it and they're also giving an example of how you can bring about that kingdom of love on earth, curing sick people, taking care of others, healing the body and the spirit of the people."

REBECA: "They performed those miracles to prove the power of love, too, because they were miracles made by love."

Someone else: "Communicating not just with words but also with deeds."

I: "For them to announce the kingdom was to say that the kingdom was near. This was the central message of the preaching of Jesus. The prophets had spoken of the kingdom that would be at the end of time. The novelty of Jesus' preaching was to say that that kingdom was coming now, in his person."

FELIPE: "He ordered us to preach it, too, and to believe it. Anyone who believes society can't change, that it will always be unjust, doesn't believe the kingdom is near."

Another of the young men: "And why is it that it doesn't get established?"

WILLIAM: "You can't impose it against people's will. And you couldn't go against the laws of history. Jesus himself said he didn't know the exact date of his final triumph. He did charge us to ask for the coming of that kingdom, in the Our Father. If he ordered us to ask for the coming of that just society, it must be near."

LAUREANO: "What's near is near. If we don't believe that, we're not revolutionaries."

I: "And we're not Christians, either. And

casting out evil spirits was very important: It meant an end to the power of the devil."

And he said to them:
"Take nothing for your journey,
neither a cane nor a purse
nor bread nor money.
Take only one shirt, not two.

ALEJANDRO: "If somebody who's preparing to announce the kingdom thinks first about himself, about how well he's going to travel, and is concerned about himself, in that case he's not going to announce the kingdom of God. He's going to announce something else. And if he's mostly interested in his own affairs he couldn't do the other job."

A lady: "They were also going to preach humility and poverty, and so they couldn't bring all the comforts of home with them. They had to go without provisions, to give an example."

OLIVIA: "It seems to me that Jesus, by saying that, also wanted to tell them that none of those things were important. What they were going to wear they would find later; everything would be supplied to them. God would give it to them. The message of the kingdom was the important thing they were taking to wherever it was they were going. And food and all the rest, that wasn't needed, because wherever they went they'd find something to eat."

MARCELINO: "They were going to teach what they had heard, that we shouldn't worry

about what we'll eat or what we'll wear. But
we should seek the kingdom and its justice,
and that's why they had to practice what they
were teaching."

Whatever house you come to,
stay in it until you leave that place.
And wherever they refuse to welcome you,
leave that town and shake its dust
    from your feet
as a sign of protest against them.

OLIVIA: "It seems to me he's telling them
that because we always want to stay in a good
house, in the best house we can find. And they,
if they found an ugly little house, well, they
had to stay in it. They shouldn't go around
choosing houses. Wherever they were welcomed, there they should stay."

Another said: "But there might be a place
where they weren't welcome, where they
didn't like the message they were bringing.
And then they should leave and make a sign of
protest."

And another: "It seems to me that also applies to us, for there are people here who don't
want to hear this message. Then we have to
leave them and not insist any more."

I said: "The message that those disciples
carried has gone from town to town and has
reached us. Some have welcomed it and others
haven't, and they can't be forced to welcome it.
It has to be done freely. But we must protest
against those who do not welcome it, and that
is the shaking of the dust from our shoes: to

make them see that they are not worthy of the kingdom."

OLGA: "It's because the kingdom isn't for everyone."

ALEJANDRO: "It seems to me that the disciple has two tasks: to announce the kingdom, that is, to conscienticize, and to help others. You can't just stay with words. Sometimes or many times you do just one thing without the other: You give help to others without announcing any message, or you give the message without giving any help."

They departed, then,
and they went through all the villages,
announcing the message of salvation
and healing the sick.

WILLIAM: "It's significant that it was the villages, the little towns, that they went to. The message of salvation was for the humble and the poor. And it says 'all the villages.' None of those poor places was to be left out of the preaching."

MARCOS: "But there could have been some people there who didn't accept the message, and they had to abandon them, and not go back to those places."

There was a silence. It seemed that there were no more comments. Finally someone added: "We too have been given that power to perform miracles, and I see that we are. We are performing them. For example, our commentaries here are a miracle."

19.

The Multiplication of the Loaves

(Luke 9:10–17)

Night was approaching. Jesus had been talking all day about the kingdom of God. The
apostles said to him:

Dismiss the people,
so that they can go and rest
and get food in the villages
and the neighboring towns,
for here where we are there is nothing.

OLIVIA: "Jesus was pleased to have those
humble people with him listening to his word
and that's why he hadn't wanted to send them
away. Maybe he didn't want them to give too
much importance to food, more importance
than to his word. And those people who had
gone to seek him probably weren't thinking of
food. Maybe they didn't even feel hungry hearing his word."

JULIO MAIRENA: "The apostles think there
isn't any food, and it seems to me that that's
the way we are now. We all say we don't have
any food. But it seems to me that the problem
isn't that there's no food. It's that a few people
have it all. If it was all shared around we'd all
be eating what those few who have the food

147

are now eating, and I think we'd all have enough."

ALEJANDRO: "That's very good, what Julio says, and it's very important for everyone to realize this everywhere (I don't know if everyone here understood it clearly): that by sharing it, there's enough for everyone. Because the order that he gives them is to share, right?"

> But Jesus said to them:
> "Give them food."
> They said to him:
> "We have only five loaves and two fishes
> unless we go and buy food for all these
>   people."
> For there were about five thousand men.
> But Jesus said to his disciples:
> "Make them sit in groups of about fifty."

PANCHO: "I'm just catching on to what this means here! They didn't have enough— right?—to feed the five thousand people. But then he says to them: It doesn't matter, share it. And there was more than enough! He made them understand that no matter how little they had they had to share it. And they shared it, and with his power he made it stretch out. The lesson is that no matter how little we have we always have to give."

MARCELINO: "Jesus also teaches us that with a little we can do a lot. He doesn't look down on poverty; he uses it to change it into riches. He didn't want to make a miracle without using anything. He didn't say: 'Hell, with those rolls and those herring you can't do anything!' No, he took them and shared them so we could see that with just a little we can do a lot. Here in Solentiname what do we have? A little corn and some fish. . . . But we can make a miracle."

FELIPE: "The teaching is also that if we come together to hear the message we're not going to be hungry, because with a united people there are no problems. Maybe I won't have food, but my neighbor will. If we're together something can happen to us like what happened to those people with Jesus Christ. If we're together it doesn't hurt to share. And then we're practicing the message of God."

I said: "Felipe and his comrades have just joined in a little 'commune' to work the land in common and to live owning everything in common. They have found that this is better than the earlier Cooperative. And they are really giving us an example of what ought to be done in this country and in all of Latin America, because this is the message of God, as he says."

ALEJANDRO: "As I see it, the same thing didn't happen to Jesus that almost always happens to the church: that it's nothing but words. That we must do good and all that. But when people are hungry, nothing is done to solve the problem. Christ not only uses words, talking to them all day about the kingdom of God, but he feeds them through his disciples. He doesn't send them away hungry. Christ's gospel also feeds you. But many bishops and priests think it's only to save your soul and not to change the economic situation of society."

MANUEL (who is also in the new "commune"): "He divided them into groups so there'd be organization, so there wouldn't be abuses, so everyone could eat and so there'd be enough for everyone."

FELIPE: "It seems that's a fundamental teaching that he gives us: that that's the way the world ought to be. That that's what his followers ought to do when he has gone, that we ought to organize ourselves in communities."

JULIO MAIRENA, who is not in the "commune" but is their guest: "If the whole country was organized like that in communities, not just fifties but thousands, it would be very different, I tell you."

ALEJANDRO, who is the leader of these boys: "He tells it to his disciples because the ones that are most aware are the ones that have to give to others. And they have to be generous and not worry about whether they have or don't have or how much they have but give all they have as was done in this case."

FELIPE: "A lot of people think things are the way they are because God wants them to be that way. He made people rich and poor, and until he wants it nothing's going to change. That's what they say when we talk to them about socialism. And that's not true. He's given us the order to change things. We have to feed the hungry, and God will give us the power to make miracles as he gave it to his disciples."

OLIVIA: "I find that all Christ's words and deeds were to teach us about life. Here he shows us that we all must do the sharing and make the increase of the five loaves that were so few, and that is to share love. Julio said it very well: Food and medicine are abundant in the underdeveloped countries, but in the hands of the poor nothing is abundant, and that's because love is lacking. The first thing is education, as Fidel says, the education of the people so that with education we can receive knowledge, and transmit it to others. And I see now that if we have that knowledge with love, then there is food, there are medicines for everyone. In these countries people die because of lack of food and medicine. The poor people don't have them due to lack of love. When there is brotherhood among everybody, it seems to me that then the miracle will occur, and then nobody will be in need of anything, because the people will be giving things through love. And that is what Christ wants, that is the kingdom of God."

ESPERANCITA, Olivia's daughter, pregnant with her first child: "The thing about the fish, Ernesto, and the loaves that were so small and they increased and got bigger, right?: that can also be a community that's born tiny and grows and gets to be big because inside it consciousness is growing and love is growing and

it gets to be the size of the whole country. I see
that in the number of loaves and fishes that it
says."

Then Jesus took the five loaves and the two
  fishes.
Looking up to heaven he gave thanks to God
and after dividing them up
he gave them to his disciples
so that they could share them
among the people.

ALEJANDRO: "Applying it to the country, I
see it this way: It's like a person that comes
and says to us: 'Look how the people are starving to death and there's a little social class
that's got everything.' And then all you have
to do is take action."

WILLIAM: "This has always been called the
Miracle of the Multiplication of the Loaves,
but I see that the gospel doesn't mention multiplication or miracle. It just says that they
shared them. Then Alejandro's applying it to
the country isn't as symbolic as you might
think. It must be that there was bread for
everyone, man, and it was all in the hands of
four or five bastards. The miracle was to persuade the owners of the bread to share it, that
it was absurd for them to keep it all while the
people were going hungry."

I said: "Could it be, then, that the apostles
distributed that little bit that they had, and
loaves began to come forth, and some people
began to pull other things out of their pockets

and bags, and there was enough for everybody, and even some left over?"

TERESITA: "Land reform is a sharing like the sharing of the loaves: A piece of land that isn't producing much is divided up and changed into great wealth that gives to everybody."

OLIVIA: "Where they have land reform, not like here where all the good land belongs to the big landowners and they won't give it up. They offer you mudholes, bogs that are no good for anything. But if there's land reform in a country, that's a miracle, a sharing of loaves."

I said that it has always been pointed out that the words used here are identical with those used at the Last Supper: "Jesus took the bread in his hands, gave thanks to God and after breaking it he gave it to his disciples."

DONALD: "It seems like he wanted to remind them of what he'd already done before, and he wanted to make them see it was the same thing. The only difference is that that time, the last time, was for them alone, while the other time the gospel says: 'He gave them to his disciples so that they could share them.' But now also he's giving that bread so they'll share it with others, and so they'll show the others what he had done before. Because at that moment with so many people, the people weren't going to catch on to what he did, and many of the people who got the food maybe didn't even find out how it happened. He wanted this to sink in, that last time."

WILLIAM: "But continuing with the supposition that there was a distribution of what was owned by certain people, who were persuaded that they ought to share with the rest, and knowing that at the Last Supper he gave thanks for his self-giving to others, and for the self-giving of his disciples: We can suppose that the first time he also gave thanks for that other self-giving and for the sharing that was done there, everybody dividing up their food in common. He gave thanks, then, for that communion."

I said that Eucharist is a Greek word that means "to give thanks." If you go to Greece you find that the word used in the street to say thanks is *Eukaristo*. I said also that in the Bible to give thanks to God, to praise God, or to bless God is all the same and that's why in the gospel it says alternately that Jesus at the Last Supper, with the bread and the wine, "gave thanks" or "blessed." In the Bible those thanks or praises or blessings were generally for a liberating action of God, of the Yahweh that always appeared as Liberation, and they were in the form of poems or songs: It was like singing of liberation. And at that supper for five thousand people, the thanksgiving, as William said, was the same as at the last one because of the same liberating event of God, the manifestation of God as the union and communion of all people. In this supper Jesus broke the bread and divided it so that all could share it, so that all could be in a common union or communion. He said later, at the other supper, that the bread was his body. His body was that communion. When we are all united in communion we are Jesus. In this gospel that we're hearing it says that earlier Jesus had been talking to them all day about the kingdom of God. He must have been talking, I think, about that communion of all people: "The kingdom of God is like a banquet . . . "

All ate and were filled;
and afterwards they filled twelve baskets
with the bits that were left.

OSCAR: "When there is a true community there is equality among everybody. Everybody ate the same, everybody was filled. That ought to happen in our country. In our country there are a lot of us who are hungry. Nobody would have to be hungry if everything in the country belonged to everybody. But here things are the way the devil wants them to be. The devil, who is the Evil One, wants us to be split apart, each one separated by selfishness. But if we all organize the way God wants, I'm sure that nobody would go hungry, because there's enough of everything in the country. There's plenty of food."

OLIVIA: "There'd be not just food left over, like there was there, but medicine, too. But now there are so many of us who are sick, and even dying, because there are no medicines to heal the poor. There are lots of medicines in the country. But they're in the hospitals. For poor people there are no medicines. They won't give them."

FELIPE: "I think that in our country there's

plenty, plenty of everything. In our country there's food, there's clothing, there's medicine, there's everything you can want, there's enough. What's wrong is that people have all that stuff not to share but to sell. And the ones that have the things want them to be scarce to earn more even though the people are starving. If you put an end to selfishness there'll be plenty of everything. There'll be education, housing, and produce, a whole lot of eggs, a whole lot of milk and meat, and there'll be lots of teachers, doctors, nurses, facilities so that kids can study for the professions they want. It'll be the multiplication of the loaves and of everything."

REBECA: "He was showing them what love could do in the world, that everybody would have enough. Through his miracle there was enough for everyone, everyone ate, and there was some left over. And that would be the miracle that love would perform in the world. Instead of the situation that we're in, when one person eats and the other doesn't. Selfishness is to blame for the scarcity of everything. Through love there'll be abundance for everybody. He performed that miracle so that we could see what love can do."

I said: "On several occasions the gospel tells us that the disciples 'had not understood' about the loaves. We may ask: What hadn't they understood? It couldn't be that they had not understood that it was a miracle, because they did take it as a miracle. It seems to me that perhaps they 'had not understood' because they understood it only as a miracle to feed many people (and as it has frequently continued to be understood) and not as a communion that had taken place there, and a communication of wealth, a distribution of things held in common. This was also a likeness of the community that we shall be in the future, when we shall all be one and all things shall be in common. In Greek there is a single word, *koinonia*, for the Eucharistic communion and for the communion of wealth, the commonwealth, and it's because for the first Christians the two things were the same. Saint Paul says that to place wealth in common is the sacrifice that pleases God, and that is like saying that perfect communism is the true Eucharist. It seems to me that that is why Christ gave thanks or praised or blessed God when he gave out those loaves and when he communicated to us his love and his self-giving together with those loaves, as William says. We have spoken here of community and communion and communication of wealth and commune and communism. What all this means (and this is what the disciples probably didn't understand) is that we are called upon to form a humanity with a unity of people, a society in the image of the Trinity."

20.

The Mother and the Brothers of Jesus

(Mark 3:31–35)

We read that Jesus was talking to the people and they told him that his mother and brothers were outside and were looking for him.

> *But he said to them:*
> *Who are my mother and my brothers?*
> *Then, looking at all those who were seated around him, he said:*
> *"These are my mother and my brothers.*
> *Because anyone who does the will of God, that one is my brother, my sister, and my mother."*

ESPERANZA, who had just married, said: "He wants us to love everyone the same as we love our family. The ones that were inside with him were like his family. He doesn't want us to devote ourselves just to our own families but to treat everyone the same."

TOMAS: "That means that he wasn't with his

158

family. It seems to me that he was far away
from them. And his mother wasn't with him,
see? So she came to look for him with all his
brothers. When they notified him, then, he
certainly sent for her so she could be with him.
It seems to me that's the way it must have
been. As soon as they arrived I suppose he
must have said that they should ask her to
come in. She'd stayed outside the church, so to
speak, because they were gathered like us
here. She hadn't come in. That's why someone
told him they were there. And then he probably made them all come in to be together, she
and all his brothers together with the ones
that were already inside, all together like a
single family. And so they'd all be gathered
there. Like in this place right here where we
are, we're all one, don't you think? That's what
I think he explained to them when his family
came to speak with him."

OLIVIA: "I see one thing very clearly and
that is that it's not enough to hear God's message; we have to put it into practice. Everybody who works for the common good of all,
that's who is a brother and a mother of
Christ."

And ALEJANDRO, her son: "There's a good
lesson here for us, who are so very close to our
families. There are people who are always defending their family, even though it does
something bad, right?—just because it's their
family. And it shouldn't be like that. You can
have a relative who's a son-of-a-bitch. And

sometimes you're more of a brother to a stranger that maybe you just met, than to your real brother who is very alienated."

FELIPE, Tomás's son: "It seems to me he meant that his mother and his relatives were the same to him as the people who were around him and followed him. All of them were for him equally a single family."

MANUELITO: "And there was no need for him to go to see his family who were outside, because the ones who were inside were also his family. It's as though he said: 'My family are here too, and I can't leave them.' "

GUILLERMO: "And I believe Christ sees that the ones that are inside there with him are exposing themselves to danger with him. And that's why he says, looking at the people who are seated around him: 'These are fulfilling the will of God; they're in this struggle with me too.' "

LAUREANO: "Jesus has a very revolutionary attitude here I believe, because every revolutionary has to break loose from his family. We have the example of Che. His family was living in Argentina and he was fighting in Cuba. Those people were his brothers too."

I remembered what had already been said on another occasion about Che: that a woman once wrote him from Spain asking him if they were relatives, because she was a Guevara. And he answered that anyone who took to heart any injustice committed anywhere in the world was his brother.

And GLORIA (who is also a Guevara) said: "He spoke there like Jesus."

I said we could think also that some of those brothers of Jesus who came looking for him were alienated people. Why not? He could have had cruddy relatives, too, couldn't he?

ALEJANDRO, Gloria's brother: "He probably had some."

I said there was a passage in Saint John where Jesus' brothers insisted that he go to Jerusalem to get publicity, and John added: "The truth is that not even his brothers believed in him." And Mark had said they thought he was crazy.

GUILLERMO: "Many of those people who were his family were the ones who afterwards left him alone, dying, covered with flies."

And another Guevara (DONALD, brother of Alejandro and Gloria): "Here he also shows them that the family is not just a single thing. We usually think that the family is only one, we can only have one family. But there can be many other people that you're united with, and they're family too. But not everyone, right? Because there are some bastards that, even though they're your blood brothers, they're not in any way united with you. He makes us see that our family can become bigger. One of us will maybe go somewhere else, and the family will say: 'He left us all alone here.' And he goes off to do something for other brothers. The way Che left his land and went off to Cuba and left his family, and maybe a girl in tears, and who knows what else. And maybe they thought he was goofing off, wasting his time. But you see what he went off to do. He did for other people even more than what you do for your family."

And OLIVIA, the mother of Gloria, Donald and Alejandro: "It seems as though he's telling us that we're all one family. When we all struggle for a common ideal for everyone, that's a single family. Christ really came to create a single family, and what has divided us is selfishness, sin. Everyone who does the will of his Father, that man is his brother, that woman is his mother. But if I'm a bad woman, I don't want my children to see me as their mother. If I do evil, I want their family to be people who work for the good of all."

FELIPE: "He thought, it seems to me, that the people who were close by him needed him more than his mother and his brothers. Maybe they wanted to see him just to say hello to him and chew the fat, asking him how he was doing and how he was feeling. He preferred people who needed more. And I believe that now that's what we have to do, because at times parents maybe need less than other people from other families who don't belong to you at all. And they're our brothers too."

I said that it seemed that this happened in "the house" of which at other times the gospel spoke, the house of the community of Jesus. And this reminds me of some young people in Managua who left their families to live in a separate community (like the community of Father Molina and Fernando, my brother). Some of them came from very rich families and left home because they didn't agree with that life and that mentality. They have gone to another family, the family that Jesus said were his mother and his brothers.

WILLIAM: "And when they rejected their families they also rejected their class. What Jesus says about families must also be understood about class ties."

CESAR: "Here we see that it's his blood brothers and his mother who arrive. But he says that they aren't his family, that his family are the ones who are with him fighting for the cause for which he is fighting."

TERESITA: "He didn't say: 'This isn't my family.' Because the Virgin was always a revolutionary. She was also his family. He wasn't excluding Mary, his mother."

OLIVIA: "What it means is that he's as interested in those people as much as in his mother. His mother and his brothers were outside like the other people he was conscientizing there. And she didn't resent that because she wasn't selfish. She didn't want her son all for herself. And we, even we poor are often selfish. We often want our children to devote themselves exclusively to us. And the rich are so selfish that even though their children are rich, they leave them their wealth when there's so much poverty everywhere."

I said that some thought that maybe Mary

and the relatives came to dissuade him, to tell him not to get mixed up in all this. The gospel really doesn't say why they arrived.

OLIVIA: "Maybe they just wanted to look at him, to see him. Because he was far away, as Tomás says. Or maybe to listen to the doctrine he was preaching."

"The gospel says 'they had him called,' " someone added.

ALEJANDRO: "They sure were screwed up. . . . It was a strange arrival. Maybe there's something of this in reality. I'd never thought of it."

I said that Jesus had said that it would be necessary to abandon father and mother and brothers, and he was the first one to give us an example. And also Mary may have come to where Jesus was to tell him not to get involved. There's nothing bad in a mother's acting that way. It was a natural thing for a mother to do (and perhaps the other relatives urged her to go with them). But she would understand his words and would see that he was right. Just as every revolutionary mother understands her revolutionary son.

Another said: "As I see it, Jesus is also trying to make us see that we are all a single family. He says: 'I believe that we are all a single family . . .' "

And another: "Not all. He doesn't say that all are his family, everybody. Just the ones who do the will of his father."

REBECA: "Those who love are the family of Jesus."

21.

The Lamp

(Mark 4:21–25)

This gospel we heard at a Mass on Mancarroncito, the last and most remote island of the
Solentiname Archipelago. The Mass was at
the home of Doña Yoya, under an arbor. Fac-
ing us, a blue cove. Far away, in the middle of
the lake, the small, solitary island of Zanata,
and farther away, as if emerging from the
water, the two volcanoes of the large island of
Ometepe. We came to say Mass at Mancarroncito because it is far removed from the rest of
the archipelago, and those who live there, very
poor and with very few boats, can seldom get
to our little church.

He also said to them:
Does anyone bring a lamp to put it under a
    bushel or under the bed?
No, the lamp is put up high,
where it will give light.

I explained that 'bushel' was a basket to
measure grain, like what Nicaraguan farmers
call a *medio* or a *cuartillo*.
   FELIX said: "I think the gospel is a very high
doctrine that God has offered to humanity to

give us all light. That's why it's like a raised lamp."

Someone from Mancarroncito: "Jesus never went around hiding. That's the light on high. And we have to be like that, too. Not hide with the truth but bring it out into the light."

JULIO MAIRENA: "People who have hidden justice are the ones who hide the light. Christ came for the poor. But often the priests, because they're getting the money of the rich, have hidden this message for the poor. And that's the light under the bushel, under the grain basket. There are others who, through fear of the powerful, apply the gospel only to their private lives, and that's the light under the bed, it seems to me. The one who raises the light high is the one who protests against injustice."

FELIPE: "Not only the priests. We also hide the light. We also have the duty to preach the truth, and many times we don't speak it out of fear. And we have to speak the truth, even though they threaten us, or attack us, or kill us, as has always happened with the prophets."

ALEJANDRO: "We have come now to have this meeting on Mancarroncito Island and to comment here on the gospel. And I see this as bringing out the lamp so it will shine. People from here will also mobilize for other places, for somewhere else, carrying that light that we always have to bring out from under the bushel. Bring it out so that it will shine for everyone."

REBECA said: "The lamp is Christ. Because he said: 'I am the light.' Anyone who reads the gospel and then hides the book in a drawer is hiding the light. Anyone who reads it and then tells about it to someone else is bringing out the light so it can be communicated to another neighbor. And that's the way Christ's word is communicated, like a light from which you light another light."

FELIPE: "We make that light shine with friendship, making one island friendly with another. Putting an end to the separation and the isolation that there is on our islands. This light will give good light when we feel ourselves all united like a single island. We transmit the light to each other with friendship, with union. We communicate Christ when we communicate friendship. The light, then, is love."

OLIVIA: "Yes, when we're isolated we don't communicate the message of the gospel, which is a message of unity, of brotherhood. We brothers and sisters have to form a community of love. They followed Christ. He preached and there were crowds who followed him and there was a lot of love there among them. And we are gathered together here illuminated by that gospel."

Well, nothing of what is hidden will remain uncovered;
and there is no secret that will not be revealed.
You who have ears, listen.

JULIO: "It seems to me that this has now been fulfilled. The priests used to read the gospel in Latin, and they said things nobody could understand. But now many of us are clear about what the gospel means and about what we're looking for: What we're looking for is to be equal."

I said: "In reality this was the great secret that had to be made public at some time. The gospel was revolutionary, but what was revolutionary and subversive in it was kept hidden for a long time."

OSCAR: "Christianity means sincerity, to be clean, to love without hypocrisy. Being revolutionary is putting an end to lying. That's why Christ came, so nothing would be hidden. So there would be light. Now society lives with falseness and lies, like somebody that has their lamp underneath the bed."

Pay attention to what you hear.
The same measure that you use to measure,
God will use it to measure you also;
and he will give even more to you who hear.
For to him who has will be given more;
but from him who has not will be taken even
    the little that he has.

FELIX: "Can that be fair? I don't understand why that's so. I want it explained."

Old TOMAS PEÑA: "It seems to me that those who have, who are the rich, God gives them more so they'll increase their capital, which

for them is their life and their glory. And he
gives it to them to ruin them. And he is going
to take from the poor even the little they have
so as to give them true glory. Because the poor
are the ones who are going to follow him.
That's what he's trying to make clear, it seems
to me."

FELIPE, his son: "I think just a little different. People who are stuck on money have no
belief in God even though they think they do.
God's going to take away from these guys what
little belief they have in him, the tiny bit of
love of God. The ones that have, and that receive even more, are the ones that love. These
God is surely going to fill more with love."

Several people said they liked what Felipe
had said, that it was true. OLIVIA commented:
"That's the way I understand it. It seems to
me that the ones who have the most love, more
love will be given to them. And the ones who
have little love, all love will be taken away
from them. They will be separated from humanity so they don't get in its way."

And one of the young people from Mancarroncito: "As I understand it, the ones who
don't have any love here on earth have nothing even though they think they do. But anyone who has love is rich, and they'll be given
more. I think that's the way it is, right?"

An old man from this island: "Those who are
generous, with every service they do to others
they get richer in their generosity. They become more generous. And those who have

nothing of that get poorer and poorer. Those who are cruel, with each cruelty they get crueler and crueler."

FELIX MAYORGA: "The rich have a saying: Money creates money. And it's true that the richer you are, the more money you make. And what about us? The poorer the *campesinos* are, the poorer their harvests are. We not only don't earn, we lose. So the rich get richer and richer, and the poor get poorer. That must seem like an injustice but that's the way it is. And the kingdom of heaven is also like that, as I see it."

JULIO: "He has said that, with the same *cuartillo* or the same *medio* that we measure with, we're going to be measured, and that we'll be given even more. He means that the love that we give we receive, and we receive even more. And also the hatred or the cruelty that we give, we receive that, and we receive even more."

OLIVIA: "He also says that people who have ears should hear. The ones who listen are the ones who already have some love in their hearts, and they're given more love. The ones who don't listen (because they have nothing) will lose what little they had. That's why the ones who have the most love will increase their love, and the selfish ones will become more miserable."

I said that we had clearly seen that just as money creates more money love creates more love and selfishness creates more selfishness. I also said that this light that today's Gospel speaks of is the light we have brought to Mancarroncito, and it's the same one that has illuminated us in this reading. With this light things have emerged that were hidden, what was hidden in the gospel has been revealed to us.

OSCAR: "That is clear. It's coming out, we're all seeing what was hidden."

The noonday sun blazed in the sky. The lake was an intense blue. Some distance away, a little sail boat. And in the background, the distant volcanoes of the Island of Ometepe.

22.

The Growing Seed

(Mark 4:26–29)

We commented on this gospel in the meeting house, after a lunch of steamed fish wrapped in banana leaves, cooked by Doña Angela, and breadfruit that Octavio brought from the huge breadfruit tree on Stork Island.

> *The kingdom of God is like a man who casts*
> *seed upon the ground;*
> *he goes off to sleep afterwards*
> *and later he gets up,*
> *and days and nights pass,*
> *and the seed blooms and grows,*
> *without his knowing how.*

LAUREANO: "When equality reigns among all people, that will be the kingdom of God."

REBECA, Marcelino's wife: "Equality will reign through love, because the kingdom of God is love. Then everybody will be one. There will be no inequality or injustice, and love will grow and grow. And the more love there is the more people will love each other and join together and be united. Love is like the seed planted on good land. It grows and grows all by itself."

FELIPE: "It seems to me, Ernesto, that that business about a man sowing a seed in the earth and the seed blooms and grows all by itself is that Jesus Christ sowed love in us. Now the rest is up to us. We're the earth, and it's up to us to see that love blooms and grows and bears fruit."

MANUEL: "The sower fell asleep. It seems like Jesus Christ died and doesn't exist now. It's like he's sleeping. But the seed is in us and we have to harvest it."

MARCELINO, who, like almost all of these *campesinos*, has just sown his late corn: "It's like he's washed his hands of it already. Like the man who sowed his corn well, and now he doesn't have any reason to worry any more."

FELIPE: "It's the earth that has to take charge of that now. And the weather—the sun, the rain."

"Which is like saying people and history," I said.

REBECA: "The 'days' and the 'nights' it seems to me are the time he's giving for the kingdom to develop. He came to die, to give us an example, and he already showed what we were all going to do. And the harvest will be when he comes to raise up all his people, a united society."

QUIQUE: "I think that business about the sower going off to sleep—maybe Jesus said it because it's a thing the church has often done: lie down to sleep, because the kingdom of heaven is going to have to come. And it doesn't do anything else—except wait for it to come."

I asked what else the sower could do, once

the seed was sown. He answered: "Put fertilizer on it, weed it."

LAUREANO: "That doesn't cut the time. What that does is give good fruit."

OSCAR: "But I agree with Quique, because if I've sown the seed and I go off to sleep, I lose it. Even though it grows and grows, the weeds grow up too, and then I can lose my crop."

LEONEL: "Maybe Jesus isn't talking about a crop that's neglected, but a good crop, grown as it ought to be, one that lets the worker have some rest. The man does his work and after that he has nothing else to do except wait. And the crop doesn't stop on account of that. It goes on all by itself."

It is because the earth produces by itself;
first comes the stalk, then the ear,
then the grains that fill the ear.

Others commented: "The kingdom at first was hidden, like a seed in the earth. Later it came up weak, like a little stalk. Afterwards there are communities, which are the ears. The communities afterwards are going to be a well-nourished people. Those are the ears that are filling out."

"But look, just because the seed that is love was sown and there is a community, does that mean we should go to sleep? We've got to be alert so there'll be more produce. I get up early to look at my seed."

"You sowed it, and afterwards now you can't do anything to make it bud or grow. It's the

earth that takes charge of that. You just take
care of it, and when it's night time of course
you go to sleep. That's just what Jesus Christ
did. He sowed his word for us, and now it's up
to us—the people, who are the earth—to make
it go on growing and bring in the harvest,
which is going to be that great community."

"It will come about anyway even though lots
of people don't want that kingdom?"

OLIVIA: "I think it will, even though there
are people who are against it. The kingdom of
love and justice has to come; it's inevitable."

I said: "Like a natural phenomenon, that's
what this parable says. That just as the plant
is produced from the seed, so from the words of
Christ this kingdom on earth will be produced."

"I believe, Ernesto, that the ones that don't
want the kingdom of Christ to be established
must be the weeds that don't let the plant
grow."

"The weeds or the selfishness that's in people. But these weeds will be pulled up little by
little, and love will win out over selfishness."

"That's what I say, because look, Jesus
Christ planted the seed and it's up to him to
pull up anything that's hurting it. But the
growth depends on us, because the kingdom
won't be made by him. It will be shaped by us,
in our own persons."

REBECA: "Love is triumphing over selfishness. And in the world, love, which is small at
first, becomes big in time."

QUIQUE: "And this gospel also gives us a lot
of hope, because we see that they kill so many

who are struggling for justice to triumph in the world and they put an end to the groups. But Jesus tells us that justice is going to triumph."

I said: "And I too find this very encouraging, because it often seems to us that the kingdom takes a long time to come and Jesus tells us here that this is a necessary delay, like that of every natural process. In nature everything takes its time, whether it's the formation of the stars in the sky or the transformation of the plants and the animals, and often they are very long times. This is what we call evolution, which is slow but it is also certain and goes toward a goal. And it seems to me that in this parable it is not only telling us that the kingdom of heaven is like a natural process but that it is a part of that same slow process of the evolution of the whole universe and that its development is the development of nature and human beings themselves. That's why we can also say that the kingdom is within us, and within us it is growing and growing. Its development is everything that improves and progresses in the world. And we can also say, as Olivia said, that this kingdom is inevitable, because the world simply *has* to improve and progress. It's a natural law. And the kingdom is a process for the future, but as a process it is already present.

And when the grain is ripe
   they go out to gather it,
for the day of the harvest has come.

Several people commented: "Anyone that
has worked in the fields knows very well when
the grain is ripe and you have to get ready to
harvest it. So also Jesus will know when conditions are right for the kingdom. It's a time that
cε ʔ't be advanced, but it can't be delayed
either."

"It seems to me that when the grain is ripe is
when the people are bringing about the new
society of justice. There's a need for union, for
us all to get together, to bring this about.
When everybody is together, the grain is ripe
and it has to be harvested. Everybody together harvests it. The sower is just one man.
It says: 'A man casts seed upon the ground'
but at the end it says that 'they go out' to
gather it."

"Because it was Christ who spread the seed,
and all of us, the people, together with him, go
out to gather it. A man goes alone to sow, but if
the harvest is large he can't gather it alone.
We might say that the harvesting is done by
Christ with all the others, Christ and the people. And the harvest is love and the unity of all
of us."

"A united people, a community with an
awakened consciousness, is already becoming
a ripe harvest."

"I think it was in Cuba that the first harvest
was gathered."

I said: "They are in that process of the ripen-
ing of the first ears. It's not that the kingdom
of God has already been established, which is
the 'kingdom of freedom' that Che yearned

for. That will come when there is no longer any selfishness. But one day a society without self-ishness will come into existence, as all revolutionaries know who fight for it even though they are not Christians. And we Christians know it too if we believe in the gospel. Here in this parable we are told that, no matter what happens, that kingdom is going to be established, because the seed was sown and the earth produces all by itself."

OSCAR said: "People who believe that that society will be produced, because they have faith in others, it seems to me that even though they don't read the gospel those people are true Christians."

And I: "Seeing that the world has continued to be full of injustice, we may think that Jesus hasn't sown anything, or that he is a sower who has neglected his crop. In fact his church has often gone to sleep. But he tells us that the plant will not go on growing, perhaps through the action of those who are outside the church. And the fact that 'the earth produces by itself' perhaps means precisely that—that humanity by itself develops love, that it is a property of the earth that the seed grows. The only thing that was needed was for love to be planted in it, and it was planted. Any other comments?"

FELIPE: "I think everything is clear."

23.

Jesus Calms the Storm

(Mark 4:35–41)

These February days are very windy, and from inside the church, where we are gathered, we hear a lot of noise from the lake. This Sunday's gospel is very important to us because three days ago Iván, Bosco, and their mother had their boat capsize. They spent more than two hours out in the middle of the lake, clinging to the overturned boat, until they were rescued. The boat was found this morning near the house of Tomás Peña.

We read that at nightfall Jesus told his disciples to take him in a boat to the other side of the lake. Some other boats went with them.

And a very strong wind arose
and the waves got into the boat,
so that they were getting wet.
Jesus was asleep in the stern,
with his head on a pillow.
Waking him up, they said:
"Master! Don't you care if we're sinking?"
Then Jesus got up and rebuked the wind
and said to the sea: "Silence! Be calm!"
And the wind was calm
and everything was left completely still.

I said by way of introduction: "I have read that on the Sea of Galilee, as on our lake, the rainstorms are heavy but they stop very quickly. According to the gospel, Jesus had been teaching all day from a boat. It must have been in that same boat that they crossed the lake. The other boats probably belonged to the people who had been listening to them and who were returning to their homes. Mark says that it was already night. We can imagine that Jesus would have been very tired, and that's why he fell asleep even though the lake was so stormy."

One of the boys: "They must have been old boats, poor people's boats, and I'll bet poorly caulked."

And another (making us laugh): "Like Cosme Canales' boat."

NATALIA: "Faith is what's important. I'm thinking of that boat that sank here—the anguish of that lady in those huge waves. And I think she can't even swim, the same as me because even though I live here I don't know how to swim. It must be frightening, don't you think, to fall into the water in the middle of the lake, without knowing how to swim. And worse if you're fat, or even if you're thin. But you can have a great faith. Just as this lady, I'm sure, had great faith. Even before she got in the boat, I'm sure she prayed to God. Once before a boat sank in that same place, because the waves are very bad there. There was a lady in it and she couldn't swim, and there she was

with a baby in her arms, and she told me afterwards that she prayed to God, and she said:
'Doña Natalia, look, me with my baby in my
arms, and I didn't know how to swim. I didn't
swim, and look, like a piece of paper, like a little
feather, with my baby girl, I didn't sink.' And
two men turned the boat right side up, and
they put her in it, and she says she was with
her baby girl in the water for an hour and she
didn't sink."

One of the Guevara girls: "But the apostles
didn't have faith. They were with Jesus there,
though of course he was asleep. But they
didn't get much confidence out of having Jesus
with them in that boat."

DON TOMAS: "They must have thought he
was almost like any one of us. That's the way it
may have been. Their lack of faith made them
afraid. Then he calmed the weather and
calmed the lake, to teach them that with him
they shouldn't be afraid. And so we too must
have faith in all of us united, because in a
community there is God. And with that faith
we can make it so that in the world everything
will be better. Because he goes with us, like he
was in that boat, even though it's like he's
asleep and we don't even feel that he's with us.
He looks like he's asleep but he never sleeps."

ELVIS: "As I see it, faith is very important—the faith that we can change this world
we live in. Anybody who doesn't have faith is
screwed. These people don't expect anything
and they don't believe in anything and with

people like that you can't bring about any change."

TOMAS: "That's the way it was with them. They were absolutely lost."

OSCAR: "When Jesus woke up—he was asleep—and looked at the wind, he got real angry. I think he got angry because his disciples, even though he was there with them, had doubts. He got sore because they didn't have faith in him. When danger came they went to wake him from his sleep. But what they had was fear, not faith. They wanted to see if that man could still do something to calm the wind. Then he got sore and he calmed the wind, showing them the power he had. And so that they wouldn't have doubts, whether he was asleep or awake."

BOSCO: "I think faith is what saves you. There I was in the water. I knew that the lake was deep, but I had faith in God. 'I'm not going to drown here like some stupid bastard, without making anything of my life,' was what I said to myself. And so I kept myself from sinking by my faith, and more faith, and more faith, until suddenly Euduviges' boat came by. I didn't see it coming through the big waves until it was on top of us. But I never lost my faith. I said to God that if I wasn't going to be worth a shit I didn't care if I drowned. But if I was going to be good for anything he had to save me. I said, 'Son of a bitch, God, if I'm going to be of any use to anybody, I can't drown!' And my mamma was shocked and said, 'You're swearing!'"

Bosco's mother, Doña Chalía, still very

moved, didn't say anything, she just wiped away some tears.

BOSCO went on: "It's one thing to be inside the boat, and it's another very different thing to be outside the boat. Outside the boat, if you give up to despair you drown. Outside the boat, if you lose faith, you're really screwed."

Young IVAN: "Even though he wasn't around there, Jesus took care of us. Inside of us, he gave us courage, and he saved me from the waves."

OSCAR: "He was with you, just as he was in that boat with the disciples when he was asleep. It looked to the disciples as though he wasn't doing anything, but they were protected."

IVAN: "But it looks as though in this case he was sounder asleep than when he was with the disciples." [We all laughed.]

CHEPE, Iván's brother-in-law: "I think Jesus went to sleep on the disciples to teach them how to behave when he wasn't there."

Another one added: "When he would be sleeping afterwards when he died."

ALEJANDRO: "I agree with Chepe, and this applies to us in many other things that have nothing to do with boats or waves, in other kinds of storms that we have. The lack of love in the world, that's the stormy lake. And it's not that we're not going to have our boat overturned or suffer other misfortunes. Faith is having faith in the company of Christ, who goes with us on the stormy lake. And that's the same as saying that faith is having faith in your friend."

FELIPE, who was the one that found the overturned boat this morning: "Faith is the faith that many young people have today. It's faith in change, in the revolution. It's faith that the world can be changed by love, that evil can become good, that those angry waves can be calmed."

ALEJANDRO: "But here in Solentiname, right here and now. If some lady's child is sick with malaria, we're not going to tell her to have faith in God and the child won't die. Faith in God is also faith in people united in a community, and that faith *can* cure the child."

Alejandro's mother: "The greatest evils of humanity are due to lack of love, and God doesn't solve them personally. He does it through love among people. We used to be content with faith in a Jesus in heaven, who isn't the one who's in the storm, the one who is here with us in the person of the other, in so-and-so, in what's-her-name, the Jesus who's with the people, even though he's asleep."

Then Jesus said to the disciples:
"Why are you so afraid?
How is it that you have no faith?"
They were much frightened and they said to
*   each other:*
"Who is this man,
that even the wind and the sea obey him?"

TOMAS: "They still lacked faith. Seeing what he was doing, they still believed in other things. They didn't believe in him."

MARIITA: "He scolds them because they're

afraid and because they don't have faith. To have faith is the same as not being afraid. It's not believing that nothing bad will happen to you."

TOMAS: "If they had had faith they would have kept their mouths shut, right? Of course, they didn't know. They didn't think he was Jesus Christ."

OSCAR: "Look here, Ernesto, it seems that the disciples were stupider than us. Because they were around him and saw him and they still had doubts. But we don't see him; we only see each other, or we see him in others. And we believe, we have the faith, we have no doubts about him. Shit! They must have been really stupid."

I said: "We also see many miracles or signs —'miracle' means 'sign'—that Jesus has performed throughout history, the transformations that his word has brought about. And still we often doubt that the world can be transformed, that the winds and the waves of history can be calmed."

"That's right!" OSCAR exclaimed, and at the same time TOMAS said: "What we can do—right?—if we have love."

LAUREANO: "They could have done what Jesus did and that's why he scolded them. Because I think we too have the power to work miracles."

I said: "This reminds me of a phrase I heard Fidel use in Havana in his July 26th speech: 'Miracles are made by the people.' It might seem to be an atheistic phrase, but it isn't."

Others commented: "Maybe it's not necessarily that they should go and give orders to the waves and the wind. But they ought to have had more confidence in themselves because they were seasoned sailors."

"Not only confidence in themselves but above all in their mission, which Jesus had already explained to them. And since they had that mission they shouldn't have been such stupid bastards as to think that they were going to die in a stupid boat. He had said to them, 'Let's go over to the other shore.' They were going to preach the message of the kingdom on the other shore, and to be scared was a lack of faith in that kingdom."

"They weren't sure they were going around with the true man. That he was the real Messiah."

"I think faith isn't whether we know Christ or don't know him. It's that we have faith that the world can change, and that we have love, which is the same thing. It's not a matter of knowing God either, because who knows God?"

"The ones who love others, according to Saint John, know God. And maybe they don't call themselves Christians," I said.

"And the Christian who doesn't believe in change is a Christian without faith," commented someone else.

OSCAR: "Everything is in getting together. Together we can work a lot of miracles."

Another: "Many misfortunes are due to the people themselves, even shipwrecks, like the wreck of the *Maria Guadalupe* that sank because the captain had it overloaded. Not to speak of the sicknesses that can be cured and many other setbacks that we shouldn't blame on God but on people."

TOMAS: "Blame them on ourselves."

I said: "On ourselves or on others, right?"

FELIPE, Tomás's son: "On others!"

TOMAS, deliberately: "On everybody. Because the fact is that if we don't speak nobody can understand. Only when the people insist can things be understood. That's why it must be us."

ADAN: "I think that now a lot of people don't believe anything. Maybe even most people. Even the most religious people, they don't believe either. They are absolute unbelievers, I've seen it. They say you can't make any changes here. And many talk against it. They have no faith."

OSCAR: "This change in people is made by people themselves, like just now the miracle of their rescue in the middle of the lake. God did it with Euduviges' boat that all of a sudden passed by."

ELVIS: "Then we're going to have a society the way the lake got that time with Jesus. The wind calmed down and everything was absolutely quiet."

TOMAS: "The fear ended and they felt liberated."

At this point I made an observation I had read in a theological article. The words of Jesus after he had calmed the lake—"Why are you so afraid? How is it that you have no faith?"—are out of place, because the disciples no longer had any reason to be afraid if the storm had passed. Those words don't seem to have been said by Jesus but were said much later to other disciples, those of a Christian community, a persecuted community, who were gathered to hear the story of the gospel and were commenting on it as we are commenting here. They applied those stories to their situation at the time and they adapted them to the new circumstances, as we do here. And sometimes the commentaries came to be part of the gospel. In this case it was a commentator who encouraged the community not to be afraid. We can't know the details of what happened on the lake because the stories were modified by the readings of the first communities. Undoubtedly something once happened with Jesus on the lake, in a boat. There are very realistic details that were engraved on the memory of a witness: the fact that Jesus was asleep in the stern with his head on a pillow (maybe just some rope), and the fact that there were other boats crossing. There may have been a squall. He may have calmed their great fright. But this dramatic story of the storm stopped in an instant was created for a frightened little community, and the words of Jesus are meant to take away their fear. They are no less now for us, and this is what is important in this gospel—not what happened once on a stormy lake in Galilee.

BOSCO: "We are now travelling in that boat. The oppressions, that's the overturn, right? But we've got to feel safe, because Jesus is in the boat with us, even though he's asleep in the stern."

COSME, the boatman: "We're going through a squall of injustices. The inequalities are the waves that are rising and falling."

TOMAS: "Our boat is filling with water and we can't bale it out. But then we have to call out to Jesus, and that means getting together. If we all get together and think: 'We're going to do such and such,' we can do anything. But if I say one thing, you say another thing and somebody else says something else, then we don't get anything done. If we all agree on doing something, it'll get done quickly, no matter what it is, because he'll be right in the middle of us to make the miracle. If he wasn't in the middle of us we wouldn't be doing anything here, and none of us would be speaking, because his word is the word we speak. Lots of times we don't come here because we have to do other things or because we don't have a boat, but we always have the desire to get together. If we didn't we wouldn't have faith in Christ or any trust in him."

FELIPE: "The storm is the attacks of the enemies of this gospel message. And we shouldn't be afraid. We must have faith, as Jesus said that time to the men who were in a boat with him."

OLIVIA: "He travels with us in the community. The boat is the community."

24.

The Possessed Man of Gadara

(Mark 5:1–20)

While we shared this commentary, the lake was very rough, as it usually is in the February winds.

We read that Jesus crossed the lake in a boat and landed on the other side in Gadara. I said that this was a city of the Decapolis, a confederacy of ten cities with a predominantly pagan population, of Greek origin, located around the lake. There a possessed man came out to them; he seemed to be a raving madman. The expression "God Most High" that he used appears in the Bible mostly on the lips of pagans.

This man lived among the graves
and no one could keep him tied,
even with chains. . . .
He went around all the time
day and night through the hills
screaming and cutting himself with stones.
But when he saw Jesus from a distance,
he ran and knelt down before him
and shouted to him:
"What do you want with me, Jesus,
Son of God Most High?
I beg you for God's sake not to torment me."

OLIVIA: "It seems to me that the possessed man would damage a community a lot, and Jesus wants to drive the devil out of him so that he'll leave the people in peace. Then the devil would feel like a failure. He was very happy making war on society. And that's why he didn't want to be driven out."

Another said: "A man with a devil inside him is a danger for everybody else. And he's a great problem especially for those who are closest to him, parents, wife, children."

And another: "He was probably a fellow with problems, who probably hated other people and hated himself."

FELIPE: "People who withdraw from a community, or make war on it, are also people who have devils inside them. And those people don't want Jesus to get involved with them. Those people don't come here and they don't want others to come."

MANUEL: "All the ones who are against the message of Jesus, which is the message of the unity of all people, they're saying the same thing: 'Don't come around bothering me, we're just fine here.' "

MARCELINO: "It seems that the man is not innocent, because he acknowledges that Jesus is the Son of God and he doesn't want him to approach. But the one who was talking wasn't the man. He says: 'Don't come bothering me,' and Jesus wasn't coming to bother the man. He was coming to bother the impure spirit. It was the spirit that was talking. When the spirit left him the man was all right and he wanted to follow Jesus. The man was really a good man."

JULIO: "Just like the worker and the *campesino* often look like they don't want to be liberated, but they're not the ones that don't want to. It's because the demon of exploitation inside them makes them talk that way or feel that way."

FELIPE: "The demon can be the selfishness that's in the heart, and when somebody talks like that it's because of selfishness. I'm convinced that selfishness is the worst demon you can have inside you. We're not the same as our other selfish side, and Jesus comes to free us from what isn't us. He doesn't come to bother us. He comes to bother our selfishness."

Another said: "The demon of selfishness makes us withdraw from others, like that man that wandered around deserted places."

And another: "His madness was also to wander around the graves because death attracted him. He preferred the dead to the living, and there are people who have evil spirits that hate life and love death."

OSCAR added: "That's right! He was a walking dead man. A man that likes to live alone out there in deserted places is dead."

And another: "Look, Ernesto, I'm also thinking that the impure spirit can be when the man is stuffed with money. He has lots of it and he wants more. And we have to drive out that demon of selfishness that he has inside him, as Jesus Christ did. The evil spirit is exploitation. They call us Communists when we

talk to them about equality and brotherhood,
and they don't want us to come near them,
because they don't want to be our equals.
Jesus did that with the demon so we'll have
courage and so we'll do the same with those
who don't want the community of all people."

And Jesus asked him:
"What is your name?"
And he answered:
"My name is Legion,
for there are many of us."

Several young people commented: "He
means that the demon was powerful and that
there were quite a few of them. There were
heaps of them!"

"Maybe he wanted to tell Jesus that the ones
that hated were an army. They hated others
and they hated themselves."

"I think maybe it's because all evil spirits,
pride, selfishness, hatred, greed, they are all a
battalion."

"On the other hand, the one who came to
drive them out was only one."

"He's saying that there are many of them," I
said, "and also that they are *legionaries*,
which is like saying 'Green Berets,' that they
are made to kill."

OSCAR: "It's true that they're well disci-
plined and very powerful, but if we get together we are stronger than they are. Because
Jesus was alone and yet all by himself he
humiliated them and made them get out and

flee. And if the people get together with Jesus, no matter how powerful the devils are, the people can defeat them and make them flee. They have no strength against Jesus—against the united strength of all of us, who are Jesus."

NATALIA: "But one man alone or one woman alone can't stand up to a whole battalion of devils."

We then read that the spirits asked Jesus to let them enter the pigs, and he let them:

> *There were about two thousand pigs*
> *that threw themselves over a cliff*
> *and fell into the lake, where they drowned.*

NOEL, an agronomist who is visiting us, said: "Did Jesus perhaps want the man to be free of the demons even though the pigs were lost and that farm was damaged?"

I said that we must keep in mind that Jews couldn't eat pork because the pig was considered an impure animal, and the breeding of pigs they considered to be illegal. I don't know if that applied also to those cities that were mostly pagan.

MARCELINO: "He sends the demons into the pigs to make us see that the demons are impure and they shouldn't be in people. Not even the pigs accept them, and they drown."

Others commented: "It wasn't pigs that were important to Jesus, it was people."

"Yes, because Jesus didn't want a reign of pigs but a reign of people. That's why he didn't care if the pigs were lost."

"Besides, he wasn't doing any harm to the community. He was doing it good when he drove out that spirit that was damaging everybody. Notice that even the pigs went mad and threw themselves into the lake."

OSCAR said: "Those bastards must have been capitalists. They were only interested in screwing the public with their business. It didn't matter to them that the man was cured. All that mattered was that they lost a lot of money, I think."

NOEL, the agronomist: "That kind of thinking goes on even today. You ought to see how the capitalists take care of their pigs and their pedigreed bulls, and they couldn't care less if *campesino* kids are starving or sick or dying. And you ought to see how they're poisoning the people with their insecticides."

An old man said: "A friend of mine was telling me that over on the other shore there were a bunch of families on some land that belonged to Somoza, and one of his men came and put a lot of cattle in the bean fields that they'd sown and he didn't care anything about those families."

And people came to see what had happened.
When they came to where Jesus was,
they saw the man who used to have the evil
    spirits in his body
and who now was sitting
dressed and in his right mind;
and they were afraid.

OLIVIA: "Instead of being glad! Because it seems to me that in a community when someone who was sick isn't sick any more that's a joy. If there is love there is joy when you see your friend well and healthy. It's logical that there should be surprise but also satisfaction. But fear ... that's very peculiar. It seems to me like selfishness."

TOMAS PEÑA: "It seems that there must have been more demons there, and that's why they were afraid and they wanted Jesus to go away."

FELIPE, his son: "People are often afraid of the word of God because they don't know it. Among us the word of God is often feared, not through ill will but through propaganda, through what they say about 'communism.' The same thing could have happened to those people. Since some of them saw that others were afraid, they also were afraid. Even without having demons they were afraid because they were seeing others who did have demons and who were afraid."

Another said: "There are many humble people among us that maybe are good, but we're scared."

FELIPE went on: "We don't have to look very far. Here in Solentiname we have humble people who are good but they're scared of change. It's the fear of communism that the propaganda of those in power has put into them. That's why there are so few of us gathered here."

I said: "Not only the simple people. The pro-

fessionals and the intellectuals are also deceived. Every day they read the capitalist
papers and they believe everything they read,
without stopping to think how those news
stories get written and who writes them."

And those who had seen it
told them what had happened to the man who
had the evil spirits,
as well as to the pigs.
Then they began to beg Jesus to go away from
their land.

COSMITO the boatman (with the big smile
with which he always talked): "I figure how it
must have been. There was a herd of pigs
around there that suddenly went crazy or
something and went off in a stampede and
since there was a cliff they all fell in the water.
Since some guy had just been cured who said
he had an army of devils inside him and since
there were a lot of pigs, people thought that
bunch of devils had got into them. But this has
helped us see that devils are pigs."

JULIO: "And also that the healing of a man is
more important than two thousand pigs."

One of the Guevara girls: "They want Jesus
to go away because they see he has great
power, and they don't know if he's going to use
it for good or for evil. They don't have confidence in him even though they see that he's
driving the demons out of that land."

OSCAR: "They wanted him to go away because they knew the great power there was in

that man who was curing those sick people. They knew what they were doing in their exploitation. Maybe it was even their fault that those people were sick and crazy."

Another: "But nobody was exploiting that mad man."

OSCAR: "Of course they were! It was their fault that he was that way. Look here. If some rich bastard is exploiting me all the time and taking everything I make away from me, maybe I'll go crazy."

I said that it was true, that mental illnesses almost always, in the last analysis, are due to social conflicts. If we didn't have these great social unbalances we wouldn't have unbalanced individuals either. That fear that they had, as Oscar said, was the fear that freedom inspires in many people. But the man who had been freed didn't have that fear.

When Jesus entered the boat
the man who had had the evil spirits
begged him to let him go with him.
But Jesus would not let him.
He told him:
"Go home to your family
and tell them all that the Lord has done to you
and how he has taken pity on you."

"Surely because of that illness, that madness of his, he had left his home and had neglected the support of his family. And Jesus sends him to his family because they need him and also so that he can take them the message."

"And Jesus had to leave in the boat, but he leaves him there to persuade those people, who were very selfish. They were afraid because they were so selfish."

"He had to leave because he couldn't stay just in one place. He was interested in other places, but he left one fellow there to hand on to others what he received. Here in Solentiname also he has given something to us not only for us to have but so we will hand it on."

"But we must begin with our own homes. My wife says to me: 'What are you going to do in that stupid church?' Well, if I can't win in my own house, how am I going to win in other houses?"

The man went away
and began to tell in the cities of Decapolis
all that Jesus had done for him;
and all were amazed.

OLIVIA: "Jesus tells him to tell what God has done for him. He didn't tell him to talk about Jesus. But the man told what Jesus had done for him. Perhaps because he realized that Almighty God was now a man; he was Jesus."

ELVIS: "Jesus told him to go to his family, but he went to all the cities. Maybe because now he felt all people were his brothers."

I said: "Perhaps Jesus didn't take that man because he was a pagan, and Jesus' mission, during his lifetime, was confined to Israel. But that man stayed there as a sign of the transformation of that world (alienated and violent, an enemy of community, and a grave dweller) which Christ was coming to liberate from its legions of demons and also even of its Roman legions, and finally of all oppression and of all armies."

COSME: "Christ went away in the boat, but from then on there began to be a change on that shore."

25.

What Makes People Impure

(Matthew 15:1–20)

The Pharisees and teachers of the law asked
Jesus why his disciples ate without complying
with the ceremony of washing their hands,
thus breaking the traditions of their ances-
tors. He answered:

> *And why do you also break the command-*
>   *ment of God*
> *to follow your own traditions?*
> *Because God said:*
> *"Respect your father and your mother,"*
> *and "He who curses his father or his mother,*
>   *let him die."*
> *But you say that a man can say to his father*
>   *or his mother:*
> *"I cannot help you,*
> *because all that I have I have offered to God."*

I said: "Those purifications that the Jews
had were very respectable religious traditions, but we see that Jesus and his disciples
pay no attention to them."

ALEJANDRO: "It's interesting to see that

Jesus is against traditions. He criticizes the
Pharisees because they disobey God to follow
their own traditions. In our religions also
there are many traditions that aren't in accord with what God wants, that is, with love.
Then we must break with tradition, as Jesus
did, for he wasn't at all traditional."

LAUREANO: "I think we have broken with
that nonsense, because for example we attend
Mass dressed in soccer clothes, dirty, not
wearing elegant clothes like people wear in
Managua when they go to church."

MYRIAM: "What is important, according to
Jesus, is the insides of people."

LAUREANO: "Why, yes, here we can come to
church dirty, but we're pretty clean inside.
While the ones who come very elegant, maybe
they exploit people. They're all rotten on the
inside, but on the surface they're all neat and
clean."

I said that Jesus was answering them sar-
castically, giving the example of a Jewish vow
called the *corban*. With that vow possessions
were dedicated to the temple and no profane
use could then be made of them. Many times
the vow was only a verbal one and the vowers
continued to make use of the possessions. But
the dedication could be used as an excuse for
not sharing them with anyone.

MARCELINO: "And they replaced the commandment to love (even love for parents) with
a religious rite. This occurs with people who
content themselves with religious acts and
don't concern themselves with others."

OLIVIA: "And there's the tradition of giving

capital to build imposing churches, like all the
ones that the earthquake toppled in Managua.
And meanwhile these people neglect all the
living Christs who are starving. They don't
interest them. They're interested only in filling their pockets with coins snatched from the
Christs that they exploit. And what they have
left over is for the church, for a baptismal font,
or a shrine, things that really have no importance." After a pause, she continued: "Their
tradition is to give alms as though God were a
beggar!"

DON TOMAS PEÑA: "We're the ones who are
beggars."

GLORIA: "It's also their tradition to buy
statues of saints, terribly expensive statues.
That's silly, stupid . . . "

ARMANDO, the Venezuelan: "They're religious people who don't carry out God's commandment because they're religious. And I
think, too, of those bishops opposed to
socialism. They don't like socialism because
they have their own traditions, not because
they're following God's mandate."

*So you have abandoned the mandate of God
to follow your own traditions.*

LAUREANO: "Jesus makes them see that God
and traditions are opposed. And it's because
God is a revolutionary."

*Hypocrites!
The prophet Isaiah spoke well of you when he
wrote:*

*"These people honor me with their mouths,
but their hearts are far from me.
It does them no good to worship me,
for their teachings are only mandates of
men."*

I said: "The Pharisees were a kind of religious party, and they were completely religious, faithful fulfillers of all the rites and precepts of their religion. They were not intrinsically 'hypocrites' in the sense in which we understand that word, because their piety was genuine and not a mere disguise in most cases. But Jesus is always calling them hypocrites, those really religious people, because he finds that their religion, even when it's faithfully carried out, is really false, an invention of men (in the same sense that for Marx all religions are the invention of men). And he finds that their religion is also alienating. It separates them from the liberation that is the 'mandate of God' (the God that brought them out of Egypt). And it's interesting to see that here Jesus is already attacking all religious worship in general, not only the ceremony of washing hands, for he quotes that phrase of Isaiah where God says: 'It does no good for them to worship me.' The prophets had stood firm saying that God did not want worship or prayers or incense or sacrifices or fasting or chants or offerings. What he wanted was justice among people and the liberation of the oppressed. The prophets didn't call for a reform in worship or a replacement of a false

worship by a true one. They wanted, instead of
any worship, love among people. Jesus takes
up the same message from the prophets and he
repeats with Isaiah that religious worship,
even though it consists of biblical prescrip-
tions, is 'only mandates of men.' "

> *Then he called the people to him*
> *and he said to them:*
> *"Listen and understand:*
> *What goes into man's mouth*
> *is not what makes him impure.*
> *It is rather what comes out of man's mouth*
> *that makes him impure."*

I said that in Leviticus and Deuteronomy
there are long lists of all the animals, pure and
impure, those that could be eaten and those
that couldn't be eaten. But we see that Jesus
corrects even the Bible. Precepts that appear
in the Bible as if given by God are, according to
Jesus, purely human precepts.

LURIO: "And we must notice that he doesn't
say we have to fulfill those precepts and *also*
the precept of love. He is simply against all
religious precepts (because I think that what
he says about food is only an example), against
all precepts which are not the precept of love."

> *Then the disciples approached Jesus*
> *and they said to him:*
> *"Do you know that the Pharisees were of-*
> *fended when they heard what you said?"*

MANUELITO: "They are angry because Jesus is bringing a social revolution. That talk of love was incompatible with a slave society. And they were content with religion."

But he answered them:
"Any plant that my heavenly Father has not
*   planted will be uprooted.*
Let them be;
for they are blind leading other blind."

REBECA: "The blind are the ones that have no love."

FELIPE: "I believe the plants that his Father has not planted are all the religions invented by human beings, which are going to be uprooted by the revolution. The only religion that God has given us is to love others."

GLORIA: "Those blind people who are leading are, it seems to me, the bishops and priests who don't understand Christianity, and who are wrong and who make others go wrong. They misunderstood the gospel and they've preached it badly and that's why we had a very poor understanding of the gospel until a while ago."

We saw that later Peter asked Jesus in private to explain that parable to them (which really isn't a parable) and he said to them:

Don't you understand that everything that
*   enters through the mouth*
goes to the stomach
and then is expelled into the toilet-bowl?

But what comes out of the mouth
comes from the heart,
and this is what makes man impure.
Because from the heart come evil intentions,
murders, adultery, sexual immorality,
theft, lies, insults.

MARCELINO: "It's strange that they hadn't understood that. It was so simple. It wasn't any puzzle."

ARMANDO: "It was probably because it was so contrary to their mentality. They were accustomed to thinking of pure and impure as material things, while for Jesus pure and impure are just the inside of people."

MARCELINO again: "What matters is what comes out of the mouth. And that's words. If you have love in your heart, the words are good. If you don't, what come out are words of hatred, cruel words, murderous words, words of deceit and theft. What makes people impure is not to have love."

MANUEL: "From the heart come words and from words come actions."

ALEJANDRO: "Crime, robberies, adultery, and all injustices are committed with words, and that's why he says that impurity comes out of the mouth of man. But good words also exist, and those are the words that ought to come out of us."

I said: "Jesus has told them crudely that no food stains people because what we eat we shit. Everything is pure in nature. And injustice is the only thing that dirties people and the universe. That's the only shit. According to Saint Matthew, Jesus gave that explanation in private to his disciples, and according to Saint Mark he gave it in 'the house.' It's clear that, in addition to what he preached for everyone, Jesus had some special teachings for his close friends. But we who are gathered here are also receiving now those teachings for the close friends."

26.

The Healing of the Daughter of the Canaanite Woman

(Matthew 15:21–28)

Jesus left there
and went to the region of Tyre and Sidon.

I said that this meant that Jesus left Israel
and went abroad. The gospel does not tell us
why. We may think he was fleeing. We know
that he was being persecuted. There must
have been some reason why he had to leave
the country. He goes to a neighboring country
(as we go to Costa Rica). But earlier the gospel
had told about the death of John the Baptist
and it said that when Jesus heard the news he
went away in a boat, to a place apart, although
many people followed him there. Now we find
him among the pagans.

And a Canaanite woman
who lived in that region
came to Jesus crying:
"Lord, Son of David,
have pity on me!

*My daughter has an evil spirit
  and suffers terribly."
But Jesus gave her no answer.
Then his disciples begged him:
"Pay heed to her,
  for she comes crying after us."
Then Jesus said:
"God has sent me only to the lost sheep of the
  nation of Israel."
But the woman approached
and knelt down before him, saying:
"Lord, help me!"
And Jesus said to her:
"It is not right
to take bread from children
and give it to puppies."*

JULIO: "He behaved very badly."

MANUEL: "He was too burned up."

ELVIS: "It seems to me that when the woman made that plea to Jesus, he didn't like it. He rejected it. Why? Who knows?"

LAUREANO: "She must have been a rich old woman."

JORGE, a young Chilean who was visiting us and who had fled from his country soon after the military coup: "She must have been an oppressor. The children must have been the children of Israel, the oppressed, and she probably belonged to the oppressors, which is why he calls them dogs."

I said that the region of Tyre and Sidon, which was also called Phoenicia, was the nation with the best developed commerce in antiquity. The Bible says that its merchants were princes. It was a very rich nation and therefore very oppressive. The gospel doesn't say that that Phoenician woman was exactly a rich old woman, but it calls her "Canaanite," and to Jews "Canaanite" was the same as saying "pagan," and "pagan" was the same as saying "oppressor." The Jews also called pagans "dogs" while the Chosen People were called "children of God."

OSCAR: "There the woman is, humiliated, right? She's humbled. She knelt down to him besides. She might belong to a people of exploiters, but she got down on her knees begging his pardon. Because she says to him: 'Yes, Lord.' "

JORGE, the Chilean: "I don't think the woman herself was an oppressor. She may have belonged to the nation of oppressors. But she also needed Christ, because she had a sick daughter."

I said: "She believed in him as a Messiah, but she knows that he is the Messiah of another people, and she addresses him with the Jewish Messianic title 'Son of David.' He explains that he has been sent only to the lost sheep of Israel."

FRANCISCO: "And the woman wasn't a lost sheep?"

CHEPE: "She wasn't from Israel."

QUIQUE, the Puerto Rican student: "It gives the impression that Jesus' movement was a nationalist movement. It wasn't internationalist. Only for one nation."

Another said: "Selfish?"

I said: "I believe the lost sheep were only

those of Israel, which had been chosen for freedom and had gone astray, that is, it had fallen into the injustices and oppressions of the other peoples. The Messiah had been promised to Israel, to free it so that, by means of that freedom, all the other peoples would be free. Jesus was always conscious that his personal mission was limited only to Israel, but after the resurrection he charged the apostles to announce the Good News to all the peoples of the earth."

OSCAR: "That woman was too pushy. Their hour hadn't yet come."

Another of the boys said: "But she has a sick daughter and she can't wait."

And another: "That business about the bread is a comparison. It's the love that he's teaching here to his group. And then when she came to interrupt him so that he'd perform a miracle for other people, she was taking away what he was giving to his own people to give it to other people. And besides they had the devil there. What could you expect? The girl was sick; wasn't she possessed? Didn't she have an evil spirit? Illness was serious business!"

I said that those people possessed of the devil, or people "with an evil spirit" as this gospel says, were usually cases of psychic illnesses, which in those times were considered to be of the devil. And maybe they are of the devil. Or, according to many modern scientists, they are produced by selfishness, which is similar.

QUIQUE: "I also think that Jesus wanted to give his disciples (and he was traveling only with them, because he was apparently in flight) an example of what would later be their work: to distribute that bread among all who had faith, without regard to their nationality. And I believe that now there are many people outside the church who don't seem to believe in God, but they're struggling to give the people justice, which is like saying God. And these are like those foreigners who supposedly couldn't have faith, because they weren't of the Chosen People, according to the laws of that time. These are the foreigners, the Communists who are receiving the bread."

MANUEL: "That the others aren't receiving, the ones he was bringing it for. Because notice, Jesus was bringing his bread for his people, Israel, but he's had to flee from Israel. There they reject him. But outside his country a woman proclaims him Messiah, Son of David."

OSCAR: "It seems then as though the dogs deserved the bread more than the children, right?"

I said that Mark tells us expressly that Jesus had wanted to be incognito abroad. And I read Mark 7:24: "Jesus went from there to the region of Tyre and Sidon. He entered a house and he did not want anyone there to know him; but he could not hide. And soon the mother of a girl heard about him ... " Mark had earlier said that Jesus had been getting a

lot of attention and that many people had
come to see him, among them foreigners from
Tyre and Sidon.

BOSCO: "It's clear he was now in flight."

JORGE, the Chilean: "But we also see that he
didn't want to do any work there. He was like
in exile and he didn't want to do anything. He
wasn't supposed to do anything there."

But she said to him:
"Yes, Lord,
but even dogs eat the crumbs
that fall from the tables of their masters."

IVAN: "She humbled herself because she believed."

OSCAR: "The woman humbled herself because she knew that he hadn't been sent to
that nation, that is, to the dogs. But now the
people of Israel scorned him. And she had to
humble herself to see if she could get what
they scorned."

MANUEL: "But she accepts that they are
dogs, doesn't she? Well, of course, because he
had been sent to another nation, and she knew
that God took them for dogs. That was her
faith: that they are pagans, that the others
are the children, and that Jesus is the Messiah
of Israel."

OSCAR spoke again: "The children scorn the
bread. Then the woman thinks that maybe
they wouldn't get just the crumbs but the
whole loaf. And she was humbled because she
wanted the loaf for herself."

Then Jesus said to her:
"Woman, how great is your faith!
Let it be done as you wish."
And from that very moment her daughter
was cured.

JULIO RAMON: "The girl stopped making trouble. The devil left her."

OSCAR: "He said 'how great is your faith' because he was scolding her. He was harsh with her, then, and yet there she was, humbled. And then he accepted her into the Jewish people. He gave her the children's bread. She needed Jesus because that girl was making life impossible for them in that house."

I said: "You have to keep in mind that Jesus didn't call the pagans 'dogs,' as the Jews called them, but 'puppies,' and that is a rather affectionate expression. He might also have said it a bit jokingly to the woman, with a smile on his lips. On another occasion, when Jesus praised the faith of a Roman centurion, in Capernaum, he said that later many foreigners would come from the East and the West to sit down at the banquet of the kingdom of heaven. There are no longer dogs, only children; we are all brothers and sisters. And the bread of Jesus Christ is for all to share, even Communists."

QUIQUE: "As I see it, there are two Jesuses here: the mortal Jesus who devoted himself only to the Jews because he was a Jew, and the resurrected Jesus, who's for everybody, who's international."

27.

The Sign of Jonah

(Matthew 16:1–4)

*The Pharisees and Sadducees went to see
   Jesus;
and to make him fall into a trap,
they asked him to show some miraculous
   sign from heaven.*

TOMAS PEÑA: "I believe there were a lot of
curious people there who just wanted to see a
miracle. And there were others who didn't like
him, and if he made a miracle they were going
to say maybe it was the devil's work. And
that's why they want to trap him there. That's
why they tell him: perform a miracle. But he
wasn't going to perform any miracle. What he
was going to do was complete, it wasn't a miracle."

I asked TOMAS what he meant about its
being complete, and he said: "Well, Jesus
wasn't going to do a thing just for people to
look at it, but for it to be a complete change of
everything, and that's something that takes
more time and more work. So it seems to me."

And one of the young people said: "They

216

wanted him to declare himself in public to be
the Messiah, that is, Liberator, so they could
set the Roman guard on him. And if he refused
to do it, then he was discredited as a Messiah.
That was the trap they were setting for him, it
seems to me."

But he answered them:
"In the evening you say:
'It's going to be good weather,
because the sky is fiery red,'
and in the morning you say:
'Today the weather is going to be bad
because the sky is a dark red.'
Hypocrites! You can interpret the aspects of
  the sky
but you can not interpret the signs of these
  times."

Another young person: "There are many
Christians who don't want to get involved in
the revolution until they see in it a sign from
heaven, that is, a religious sign. But they're
not going to see more than what they're seeing, just as the Jews couldn't see any more
than what Jesus was doing, which was freeing
the oppressed and announcing the good news
to the poor."

Another added: "Since John the Baptist
there was a mass movement, which they could
interpret ..."

TOMAS: "It seems they didn't believe in
Jesus, then. They thought he was maybe a
private individual, and that's why they were

bothering him, asking him for a sign. But he couldn't do anything, because his hour hadn't come yet. He was just waiting."

I said: "And Jesus is telling them that instead of the signs from heaven that they are asking for, they are seeing the signs of the times, that is, of history. And that just as they interpret the signs of the weather (which are also signs from the heavens) they should also be able to interpret the signs of the changes in history. And it seems to me that he wants to make them realize that the signs of history are also other signs from heaven."

FELIPE: "He calls them hypocrites because they don't see what they don't want to see. And because they are religious people who are waiting for things from the heavens they don't want to see the social changes."

JULIO: "Jesus tells them that, according to them, when the sky is one kind of red there's going to be good weather, and when it's a different red there's going to be bad weather. Old people around here say the same thing. When the sun is very red, with brilliant cloud banks, they say there was a fine sun and there'll be good weather; and when it's a sad yellowy red, kind of worn out, there'll be bad weather. Isn't that so, Don Sóstenes? But it seems to me that Jesus is also telling them that because the red is blood, and it's also the revolution. Depending on what kind of red it is, we can know if it's oppression or liberation."

MANUEL: "Maybe some of them wanted to believe in him and they were asking him for a religious sign, or rather a magic marvel. And if he'd given them that sign maybe they'd have believed in him. But Jesus was getting no-where with that kind of faith. No social change was going to take place by getting them to believe in him that way."

TOMAS: For sure they were expecting some powerful man to come down, a very rich man, or maybe a dictator, and that he was going to boss the people. But then they saw him . . . A poor man! . . . And then they didn't believe in him."

ELVIS: "The fact that he was poor and was surrounded by poor people, for them that was no sign, right?"

GOYO: "Because they were self-satisfied. But for the humble and the people thirsty for justice, that *was* a sign and that's why they followed him and clung to him."

These evil, faithless people want a sign,
but they will get no more sign
than the sign of Jonah.

I said that in two other passages from the gospel there is a mention of the sign that Jesus will give as "the sign of Jonah," and two differ-ent explanations are given. According to Matthew, it's because Jonah was three days inside the fish, and in the same way Jesus was going to be inside the earth and afterwards was going to be resurrected. According to Luke, it was because Jonah went to preach in the city of Nineveh, which was filled with injustices, and he converted the whole population, from the king on down, making them all change their attitudes. I asked if there wasn't a contradiction between the two evangelists.

GOYO: "It's just one sign, and we are seeing it: Jesus has risen from the grave and he is here among us, and he is making us change our attitudes."

FELIPE: "Or he's going to make us change our attitudes. Because the real change of attitude is to change the social system."

And I said it was very encouraging for us, that sign of Jonah that Jesus announced. That conversion of Nineveh, the capital of the Assyrian Empire, a city so large that, according to the Bible, it took three days to cross it, was not a historic fact but a literary fiction. It is now known that the book of Jonah is a novel, and that Jonah was never in Nineveh, which had been destroyed long before. But Nineveh has gone on existing since, in every oppressive empire, and it still exists. And Jesus announces that he is really going to achieve the conversion of Nineveh, no longer in a literary fiction but in history.

RAUL VARGAS, a young poet from Managua: "That sign of the times of which he speaks, it seems to me, refers to the fact that Roman imperialism and slave society were coming to an end. He tells them that they must know how to interpret history, right? One of the causes of the fall of the Roman Empire was Christianity."

ALEJANDRO: "And we too must know how to

interpret the history that we are living. The signs of the times are the liberation movements in Latin America and in many other parts of the world, the social changes that are going on and the ones that have gone on in Cuba, and the fact that the poor everywhere are receiving the good news. All this is what Jesus calls the sign of Jonah."

MILAGROS, Natalia's daughter: "That sign is very clear."

28.

Peter Declares that Jesus is the Christ

(Matthew 16:13–20)

Jesus asked his disciples who people were saying that he was, and they said:

Some say John the Baptist;
others say Elijah,
and others say Jeremiah
or some other prophet.

TERE: "He saw that the people were following him, and it seems that he wants to know why."

WILLIAM: "He's interested in knowing what the people were thinking. And the people are never wrong. John the Baptist and all the prophets had denounced evil governments, right? And that's the reason the people said that Jesus was a new John or a new prophet. And the people weren't misled when they saw him as an accuser. But there was something the people couldn't yet know."

Then he said to them:
"And you, who do you say that I am?"

WILLIAM: "And he wants to see if the ones who have been closest, the ones who know him most intimately, have now realized . . . "

OSCAR: "I feel that he's now asking us the same question, in this community: Who am I in your eyes? I'm going to answer for myself, as Peter answered for himself. For me, he is one who is making me change, since I came to know him (not long ago). I was a real selfish bastard, and now, it seems to me, I'm getting to be less of a one. And he has united me with others. And he's the one that keeps us united in this community. He has brought us together. What for? To unite, with groups like this, the whole world, and to change the world."

Simon Peter then said to him:
"You are the Christ,
the Son of the Living God."

I said that "Christ" is the Greek word *christos*, which means "anointed" and is a translation of the Hebrew word *Mashiah* (Messiah), which also means "anointed." This is the first time in the Gospels that Jesus is proclaimed the Messiah. Peter is saying here that Jesus has been anointed king, and that he comes to free the people and to establish the kingdom of God.

OLIVIA: "That's very different from what the rest of the people were saying, that he was a new prophet. Because prophets used to announce the kingdom, while with Jesus the kingdom came."

ELVIS: "The kingdom began. But it's still a long way from being established throughout the earth."

OSCAR: "But that day is closer and closer, I say."

Jesus answered him:
"Blessed are you, Simon, son of Jonah,
because no man has shown you this,
but my Father who is in heaven."

TOMAS: "Because there are things that are learned through people. For example, one person can teach another person to read. But the wisdom of God only God teaches."

REBECA: "The truth is that the people couldn't know that he was the Messiah if they still weren't seeing any change. They had to think that he was just a prophet, an accuser, like there had been before. And they couldn't know either that he was the Son of God, because in the people's eyes he was just the son of Saint Joseph."

One of the Guevara girls: "It seems to me that the true wisdom is that of love, and that's why it says that that wisdom is not transmitted by men but comes from God, because God is love."

WILLIAM: "What they were seeing was that Jesus was a man poorly dressed, humble, a proletarian, and in his presence they didn't see anything that seemed to be a kingdom. But Peter understood in a mysterious way that this man was no longer a prophet but the one who was coming to fulfill the prophecies of the prophets. And Peter believed in the changing of the world. That's why Jesus calls him blessed. And we too must feel ourselves blessed, this little group here, because we too believe in the changing of the world."

"But there are many Christians," I said, "who still believe that Jesus is nothing more than a prophet, that he has come to announce a future salvation but not to bring about any revolution in the present. They believe in Jesus in many ways but they don't believe in him as the Messiah. These people, the ones who don't believe in the changing of the world, Saint John calls them the Anti-Christs, the Anti-Messiahs."

And I say to you that you are a rock, Peter, and on this rock I am going to build my church,
and not even the power of death will be able to conquer it.

I said that *Petros* in Greek is "rock," and this is a nickname that Jesus is giving to Simon when he announces that upon him he will build his church. I said also that the Spanish word *iglesia* [church] comes from a Greek word, *ekklesia*, which didn't mean at that time a religious institution but simply a gathering, or even better, what we call today a community. I also said that we were used to the translation: "The gates of hell will not prevail against it," but that "the power of death" is more exact because Jesus was not talking about hell as we understand it now, but about the *sheol* of the Jews or the *hades* of the Greeks (the region of the dead). Jesus refers to death as a kingdom or an enemy community. Among the Jews, who put walls around their cities, the word "gates" meant military power.

MARCELINO: "He gives Simon the nickname 'Rock' because he's going to build something new. It has to be on firm rock. The firm rock, it seems to me, is the faith that he is the Messiah, the Liberator, the one who's going to change the world. Our community of Solentiname must also be based on that faith. If it isn't, the same thing will happen to us that happens to religion in many parts of the country. It's like an old house that's falling down, all shattered by the earthquake."

His wife, REBECA: "A church without faith can't be a church. It's not a community. And without that faith, we really live without life; we live without any hope."

MANUEL: "He called Peter the leader, perhaps because he was the most vigorous. He wasn't a drivelling idiot. He was the toughest. Peter was tough. Remember when he tore the guard's ear off. Christ must have said: 'This is no ordinary son-of-a-bitch. I want him to be the head of my community.' "

I said: "We have read that Jesus called Simon 'Son of Jonah' (which in Hebrew is *Barjona*), but some people now think that this could have been an error in translation, because that word also means 'terrorist.' They think that that was another nickname that he used to have—Simon the Terrorist—and that probably meant that Simon belonged to the national liberation movement of the Zealots, supporters of armed struggle. That explains why, when Jesus announced his death, he was violently opposed to the idea of Jesus allowing himself to be killed. And when they came to arrest Jesus, why he would have drawn his sword."

Another of the Guevara girls: "That also explains why he had more faith in the Messiah, in the Liberator, because he was in the guerrilla movement."

OSCAR: "Standing face-to-face with this other man, he didn't hesitate to tell him that he was a Son of God, right? And Jesus noticed that nobody else dared to talk with the firmness Peter talked with. Then Jesus told him he was a rock, and that he could form a community. And it's this community of ours that must also be hard as a rock because it has many enemies."

OLIVIA, who had just lost her daughter Olguita: "And the greatest enemy is death, but Jesus says that not even death is going to prevail. It's not that none of us is going to die. Everybody dies, individually, physical death. But in community we don't die because we are in community with him, and he has conquered death. He has risen from the dead. That's why not even death can do anything against this community."

WILLIAM: "And if death can't do anything,

the other enemies can do even less. They're the allies of death."

> *I shall give you the keys of the kingdom of*
> *   heaven;*
> *whatever you bind here in this world*
> *will be bound also in heaven,*
> *and whatever you loosen in this world*
> *will be loosened in heaven.*

I said that just as Jesus had spoken earlier of the "gates" of death, he also speaks of the kingdom of God as a walled city, and he gives Peter the keys to those doors. The kingdom of God is different from the church or community that he had spoken about before. The community is to prepare for that kingdom. Whatever he does or undoes among people will be corroborated "in heaven," that is, before God. We know that Matthew often, in order not to mention the name of God, uses the word "heaven."

MANUEL: "It means that Saint Peter doesn't have the keys to the entrance to heaven. The keys of the future society of people, those are the keys of heaven."

REBECA: "The keys are love. Because the one who loves enters and the one who doesn't love doesn't enter. They aren't keys so that he can let you enter or not let you, as he chooses."

OLIVIA: "It seems that he's saying that he's giving him the keys because he's giving him a very big responsibility, a pledge to the people."

FELIPE: "He goes away, he departs, leaving

the kingdom as a responsibility of people."

MANUEL: "He's giving Peter authority. And the same way he's giving that authority to the bishops and to the priests and to all the leaders of the church. With that authority in many parts of the world they are condemning the rule of the capitalists, since many people are dying because of those same capitalists. They are defending the exploited people. And so we must support that authority, we all must, when they are in favor of the people and attack the governments, because they are speaking in the name of God."

Another young man: "And when the leaders of the revolution here in Nicaragua speak, we must support them, too, because the leaders are also speaking the truth. They also are speaking in the name of God."

MANUEL: "Well, it used to be that the bishops and the priests weren't on the side of the people. It's been almost five years, or maybe ten (I'm not sure it's that long) that they've spoken up for the people. And if they were with the oppression they weren't with the community of Christ, their church. But every leader of social change, of the coming of the kingdom of God, is also a representative of the community of Christ."

I said that the church that Christ founded upon the rock of Peter (maybe because Peter, a militant in a national liberation movement, had a firm messianic faith) was intended to create the kingdom, but the kingdom would not be the church. It would overflow it and it would cover the whole earth. And Saint Paul said that in the end Christ will deliver this kingdom to the Father after destroying all "dominion" and all "authority" (when people are entirely free), and that the last enemy to be destroyed will be death. For that reason, as Christ says, the gates of death will not prevail.

> *Then Jesus ordered his disciples to tell*
> > *no one*
> *that he was the Christ.*

OSCAR: "Maybe because he didn't want everybody following him like sheep. He wanted them to believe with a firm faith like Peter and not because they were dragged along by somebody else."

JULIO GUEVARA: "Or maybe he didn't want a lot of publicity."

REBECA: "He wanted them to know him as Peter knew him, because God enlightened them, and not because other people said to them 'That one is the Christ,' 'That one is the Christ.' "

FELIPE: "And if he had declared himself the liberator of the poor from the beginning, they would have screwed him right then and there."

I said that to be declared Messiah or "the Anointed One" (King of Israel) was doubly dangerous. First, with the people because it lent itself to false interpretations, since in those times the Jewish nationalists were waiting for the Messiah only as a king that would free them from Roman rule. And the kingdom of Jesus was for the whole earth and its freedom would be from all authority and rule and even from death. That's why he always shied away when they tried to proclaim him king. And second, with the authorities because it led to his death. In fact that's why they condemned him to death, and Pilate ordered them to write the crime (a political crime) on the cross: that he had declared himself king.

Someone said: "There are still many places today where it's dangerous to say this."

29.

Jesus Announces His Death

(Matthew 16:21–23)

Last Sunday we saw that Peter had declared that Jesus was the Messiah, and now we see what Matthew said next:

From that time on
Jesus began to explain to his disciples
that he would have to go to Jerusalem
and that the elders, the chief priests,
and the teachers of the law
would make him suffer a great deal.
He told them that they were going to kill him
but that on the third day
he would be raised from the dead.

I said: "He announces that he will be condemned by all the official leaders of the Jewish people: the elders who made up the Sanhedrin or supreme court, the high priests, and the scribes."

WILLIAM: "That always happens. Anyone who fights for the people knows that sooner or later they'll run that risk. It's always been that way, from Jesus right up to now, and even

before Jesus the same thing happened to the
prophets. And the convictions have always
come as much from religious authorities as
from political authorities. Because the religious authorities have always been allied with
the politicians, though they claim to be non-
political."

I said this was the first time that Jesus announced his death. He had spoken before of
gathering the sheep of Israel. In biblical language to be a "pastor" means to be a leader. He
was planning to begin with Israel the kingdom
of justice for all. Later, when he was weeping
over Jerusalem, he would complain that they
wouldn't let themselves be united. It seemed
that now he had realized that his message
could not be accepted either by the Sadducees,
the priestly party of the high, monied class, or
by the Pharisees, the traditionalist religious
party of the urban middle class. Both groups
felt a deep scorn, and even hatred, for the
urban and rural proletariat and therefore for
the cause of Jesus. And he had seen that he
had no alternative but to die. He would unite
humankind, but only after his death, and in
fact by means of his death. And he spoke of an
immediate resurrection. In biblical language
"on the third day" does not mean literally
three days later, but very soon afterwards,
right away.

WILLIAM: "And that business of going to
Jerusalem means that he is looking for a confrontation with the authorities. He's analyzed
the situation and he knows perfectly well what

the result will be. He's going into enemy territory. That's where the Jewish religious power and the power of Rome were. In other parts of the gospel we see that the disciples were afraid to go to Jerusalem."

A young man: "It was almost like suicide. That's why he later said they weren't taking away his life because he chose to give it."

OLIVIA: "The disciples are now sure that he is the Messiah, for after Peter spoke he told them to keep the secret. But since there was hope that the Messiah would have a political victory, he begins now to explain to them that it's not going to be like that, that his victory will be to die."

> *Then Peter took him aside*
> *and began to rebuke him, saying:*
> *"God forbid, Lord!*
> *This must never happen to you!"*

ELVIS: "I think Peter was talking there not only for himself but for everybody, and it was natural that he should think like that. They thought Jesus was interested only in ruling. And they didn't know yet that the kingdom was not to rule but to liberate."

REBECA: "They weren't thinking about others. They were thinking with selfish minds. They didn't care that others might be saved."

OLIVIA, who shocked many people by not wanting to dress in mourning when her daughter died: "They didn't care about resurrection and they pay no heed to it. Jesus says

he's going to die and be resurrected on the
third day, and all they think about is the death
and they ignore the resurrection. They really
didn't believe in it. When they think about
death, they think only about death, and not
death and resurrection as two things together."

REBECA: "Those who love, when they die
they get resurrected like Christ right away."

JULIO: "It seems Peter was the natural
leader of the group, and maybe also that's why
Jesus had confirmed him as responsible for the
community. He had a lot of pull, and he even
went so far as to scold Jesus. He started an
argument. He told him he ought to fight and
conquer, not let himself be beaten. He told him
that he shouldn't let them screw him like
that."

GLORIA: "And that he shouldn't go."

I: "In Galilee there had always been upris-
ings and guerrilla fighting. Armed resistance
was possible. Galilee was not controlled by the
Romans. But to go to Jerusalem was to put
yourself defenseless into the hands of the
enemy."

But Jesus turned around and said to Peter:
"Get away from me, Satan!
For you are an obstacle to me.
You do not think like God but like men."

OLIVIA: "He calls him Satan because Satan
is selfish. Or else: selfishness—that's Satan.
To think of sacrificing yourself for others is to

think like God. He tells him, too, that he's
thinking like men and not like God: He means
that men think like Satan because they're selfish. That's the way the world thinks. And
that's the way people think in Nicaragua.
They think about ruling, not about sharing or
giving anything to anybody. The government
we have has that mentality, Satan's mentality."

One of the young people: "You have to say to
that mentality what Christ said: 'Get away
from me!'"

And another: "Peter tells Jesus that can't
happen to him, because he couldn't suffer,
only triumph. Peter didn't know the Messiah
was a liberator. That's why Peter was an obstacle to Jesus, and to us. Otherwise we
wouldn't have been liberated, not even Jesus
himself would have been liberated."

Another: "Selfishness is always an obstacle."

TERE: "When Peter declared he was the
Messiah, Jesus told him he knew this through
God and not through men. But when he believes the Messiah mustn't suffer, there he
isn't thinking like God but like men."

FELIPE: "I believe people who think like hu-
mans are people who just think of themselves,
and those people are mainly the exploiters, the
ones who've ruled human society up to now.
People who think like God are people who
think of others, people who sacrifice themselves, people who fight for liberation. And I
believe that's the way people are divided: peo-

ple who think like men and people who think
like God."

WILLIAM: "It's very human to think like
Peter, that Jesus shouldn't let himself get
screwed. But that's not thinking like God, who
in the Bible always appears as love, the force
of life that drives people on. To think like God
is to think revolutionarily. Peter, I bet, was
afraid too. But fear comes from thinking about
yourself. Love takes away fear. Anyone who
loves isn't afraid of death."

CESAR, the teacher: "It's a temptation that
Peter presents to Jesus, and we all have that
temptation. On one side is the ruling and on
the other side is the sacrificing. Peter and the
other disciples who also sought power, and
above all Judas, present that temptation to
him. Jesus rejects it and chooses sacrifice. He
is clear about what he has to do."

I said that what César said was very sound
and I added an observation of the Jesuit Ig-
nacio Ellacuría that I had recently read: The
words of Jesus to Peter are the same as those
he said in the desert when the devil tempt-
ed him with a false messiahship of ruling:
"Get away from me, Satan!" It's clear, then,
that here Jesus was having the same temptation. And to judge by the violence of the rejection it must have been for Jesus a very strong
temptation. At the end of the episode in the
desert Luke says that the devil went away "for
some time." We know that the power of dark-
ness returned again on the Mount of Olives,
where the agony made him sweat blood. And it

is curious that it was then that he said to
Peter, whom he found sleeping, that he ought
to keep watch and pray "so that they would
not fall into temptation." This was the great
temptation of Jesus, his messianic temptation: seizing political power, as the armed
struggle of the Zealots understood it. This is
the temptation that Peter, and perhaps not
only in his own name but in the name of the
other disciples, is presenting to him. We have
already seen that Peter's nickname was "the
terrorist." There was another disciple who
was called Simon the Zealot. And the family
name of Judas, Iscariot, may have come from
the word *Sicarii*, which was another name
given to the Zealots. The fact that Jesus had
rejected this temptation—a real temptation
for him—is no grounds for condemning, in
the name of the Gospels, armed struggles for
freedom. Jesus never condemned the Zealots,
only the supporters of the status quo: the
Pharisees and the Sadducees. And he did not
condemn them in spite of the risk that he
might be confused with the Zealots, which in
fact happened, and he was condemned as a
Zealot. The only thing we can say is that Jesus
saw that his mission as the Messiah was different. We must keep in mind also that the
Zealots hoped only for freedom from the
Roman Empire and for the restoration of the
past grandeur of Israel, with a nationalism
that in today's language we would not call
revolutionary but rather reactionary, maybe
even fascist.

CESAR: "Peter has not understood the mission of Jesus and he is denying it, with a denial like the one he later made during the Passion. He didn't want to die for that cause, the cause of freedom, which was going to be the glory of Jesus and of them all. Because he didn't understand that cause, he later tried to separate himself from it. We too often refuse to sacrifice because, like Peter, we don't understand our cause clearly, and the Satan Jesus speaks about is also in us. Maybe later we'll understand that that was the road we had to follow. Just as Peter later understood that the other liberation was not the true liberation of the people or of all humanity, that the road of Jesus was the more revolutionary one."

I said that several times Jesus insisted in the gospel that he had to die. We could ask ourselves why he had to die. To say it was to save us doesn't shed much light, because we can still ask why he had to die (and not triumph) to save us. It seems to me that Paul is very enlightening in the Epistle to the Romans when he says that the Jews' rejection of Jesus was a secret plan *(mysterium)* of God, for it was the way other peoples have achieved salvation. The crime of the Jews, he says, turned out to be for the benefit of the world. The Jews hardened their hearts only in part, so that the other peoples could enter. Later all Israel will enter, and a consequence of this, according to Paul, will be the resurrection: "If his rejection was the reconciliation of the world, what will his acceptance not be? Noth-

ing less than life for those who were dead."
He means that the kingdom of the Messiah
became universal because it failed among the
Jews. If it had triumphed, given the historical
and political context of that time, it would
have been purely a Jewish kingdom, along the
lines of the nationalist movement of the Zealots. So Jesus could not triumph in Jerusalem.
He had to die in Jerusalem.

OLIVIA: "To die and rise again."

30.

Taking up the Cross

(Luke 9:23–27)

And he said to them all:
"If any one of you wants to come after me,
forget yourself,
take up your Cross each day,
and follow me."

WILLIAM said: "It's an invitation to go with him to Jerusalem."

OLIVIA: "To forget yourself is to think of others. Just as to think about yourself is to forget others. Let's stop being selfish, that's what it means to forget yourself. Jesus wants us to forget selfishness. Not just the rich. We have to forget our selfishness and change our attitudes too, because we poor people can also be selfish and think only about ourselves and not about the community."

Another lady: "To follow Jesus means not to think about yourself, the way Jesus does, to have the same mentality as Jesus. It also means to suffer for others and that is to take up the cross each day. Because to forget yourself means to sacrifice yourself, and that is to suffer. To suffer for others, of course, not to

241

suffer for yourself. Because the rich also suffer and sacrifice themselves, but not for others, for themselves, to heap up more treasure for themselves alone or for their families, who are themselves. And when the rich die they want their capital to stay right in their families. Even when they die they don't let go of themselves, and they go on being selfish beyond the grave."

One of the boys: "To get rid of selfishness, we have to practice that, we who follow him, right here in Solentiname, even though we're not rich. Because if we don't get rid of that old mentality we're not his followers and we're not revolutionaries."

I said: "The cross was a torture of the Roman state, not of the Jews, and it was a punishment for political crimes. It was the torture intended for subversives, who in those times as today were considered wrongdoers. Jesus is saying that his followers have to be subversives. Jesus is going to Jerusalem, which is occupied by the Romans (Galilee wasn't occupied). He knows what is waiting for him there as a revolutionary and he anticipates that the Roman state will condemn him for political crimes. He sees that that will also be the fate of his followers, those who want to go after him to a Jerusalem occupied by the Empire."

> *Because he who wants to save his life*
> *will lose it,*
> *but he who loses his life for my sake,*
> *he will save it.*

A young man said: "Anyone who clings to his life is screwed."

LAUREANO: "People don't want to get involved in anything so that they won't get screwed, jailed, killed. But the one who fights evil, he runs the risk of getting screwed and the one who is fighting is fighting for his comrades, for his brothers, and so he is being saved because of them."

FELIPE: "There are some people who fight to defend injustice and they are killed for defending it. And other people fight so there won't be any injustice. And the ones who die fighting against injustice, God will surely save. And the ones who die to defend injustice, they must have been already dead. That's the way I see it."

Another: "I see it this way: People who defend this system to defend their security or their money, when the revolution comes, they're going to lose everything, maybe even their lives."

I: "And they have really lost their lives already, even without anybody having had to take them away from them, because the life they lead isn't really a life. And this applies to all the selfish ones, because the life of the selfish isn't really life. They are living dead."

WILLIAM: "And this applies especially to the rich, the ones whose lives are spent just making money to enjoy life. And what they have isn't life and they don't enjoy anything. But those who give their lives, that is, those who live for others, they are the ones who really keep their lives and enjoy them and are happy, because the only happiness is love. And that life is never lost; it's an eternal life."

MANUEL: "Let's not talk just about the rich. Also in Solentiname, through selfishness or cowardice people don't struggle for the cause of freedom. And those people also by saving their lives lose them. Because there have been many centuries of exploitation, right? If we weren't cowardly and selfish, everybody would have been freed centuries ago."

Another: "Take the construction workers in Managua, who've gone on a protest strike because of the sixty-hour work week that Somoza imposed on them. They're risking their security, running the danger of being jailed. But that's the way to change their conditions, and even the conditions of all the exploited, if the strike spreads to all the workers in the country."

OSCAR: "I don't know . . . I'm very ignorant, but it seems to me that life and love are two things that are alike or maybe the same thing, I don't know, and so to live is to give your life for others, while to try to save your life selfishly for yourself is not to live, if you understand what I mean."

I said: "Oscar is quite right. Life is love. And we can see that all the life in the universe is created by love: the life of people, and of animals, and of plants."

WILLIAM: "Life and love are the same thing and the person who embraces love is the person who really lives. And the life of the selfish person isn't life. And therefore to save your life selfishly is to be in death and not in life."

LAUREANO: "I remember Che, who is very
much alive because he gave his life for others.
If he had just wanted to enjoy life, he wouldn't
be alive as he is, even though he'd still be living; or better, he wouldn't be alive as he is now
everywhere like someone risen from the
dead."

ALEJANDRO: "Jesus says, 'he who loses his
life for my sake,' and that means for the sake of
the oppressed, the sake of the people."

WILLIAM: "And this business of giving your
life for his sake doesn't have only the sense of
physical death but also of living for others.
That's also a way of giving your life. Your life
already belongs to others, so the life you give
gets lost. It's not your life any more."

FELIPE: "This is very interesting to me because the common people who won't fight for
their freedom so they won't lose their lives,
they are in fact losing their lives. Even though
they're not being shot with rifles, they're
being killed, because the life of the oppressed
is no life."

ARMANDO: "You can lose your life for love
fighting in the street, or in jail being tortured,
or in the woods, and maybe that's the way we
lose it. But there are other ways of losing your
life for love, maybe even costlier ways. That's
why Jesus says you have to take up the cross
'each day.' "

"Which is like saying you have to be subversive each day," I said.

Another: "Life is lost not only through arms.

Some are not called upon to die through arms. But anyone who loves has to suffer some death, has to know some kind of death, because of his love. That's why the gospel says that Jesus said this 'to everyone.' "

ARMANDO: "But there's something else. Even those who die in an armed struggle have already before known an earlier death, the death of their selfishness. I'm thinking now about Che, when he said in a letter to his parents: 'I have polished my willpower like an artist' (I have made my heart revolutionary). And that is to become more and more generous, more and more open, more and more humble, more and more devoted to others, and that is a death. Maybe harder than the death he met at the hands of the Bolivian army."

Another of the boys: "The ones who 'save' their lives are the ones who avoid sacrifice. But they lose their lives. Their lives are worthless."

And another: "But to give your life is really to save it and not to want to give it is to lose it."

For what good is it for a man to win
the whole world
if he loses himself or destroys himself?

A lady: "When you're dead, your wealth is no good to you, no matter how wealthy you used to be. And also if you're selfish your riches are no good to you, you can't enjoy them, because you can enjoy them only through the love of

others. And the selfish are dead even though
they win the whole world."

And a boy: "Just by winning the whole world
you destroy yourself because you become an
oppressor, a selfish person. Also the rich, just
by being rich, have already destroyed themselves, because to be rich is to refuse to share
with others. You can't be rich without being
selfish. And so it does nobody any good to possess riches because they become dead."

And another: "According to what Jesus tells
us, I see that there are two kinds of owning:
owning things and owning yourself. If you win
things you become rich but you lose yourself
and you've won nothing."

I said that I like this translation that we
have read ("what good is it for a man to win the
whole world if he loses himself or destroys
himself") better than the one we have traditionally had (" . . . if he loses his soul") because
the Jews didn't have a word "soul" (as distinct
from the body) and for "soul" they used the
word "life" (the vital principle that animates
the body). That's why the Greek translation of
the gospel uses the word *psyche*, which means
"life" rather than "soul." Because we translated into our language as 'save his soul' what
in the language of Jesus was 'save his life,' this
phrase has traditionally been badly interpreted, being understood in the sense of a
purely individual and other-worldly salvation.
But the interpretations given here seemed to
me to be very much in accord with what Jesus

meant by speaking of gaining the world and losing your life (or your person).

Another said: "But if we don't destroy ourselves but possess ourselves, if we love, and if we live united with others forming all together a single person, then we *can* possess all things and conquer the whole world and all the riches of the earth. Because then we won't want all the things just to enjoy them ourselves but so everybody will enjoy everything equally, each one equal to all the others."

WILLIAM: "What good does it do you to win the whole world if you lose your life because you don't give it up, you don't give it to others, and you want to keep it selfishly for yourself?"

> *For if someone is ashamed of me*
>   *and of my message;*
> *the Son of Man will also be ashamed of him*
> *when he comes as king,*
> *with the glory of his Father*
> *and of the holy angels.*

I said that "glory" is something that in the Old Testament is applied only to God. Jesus here says that the Son of Man (who is also, so to speak, Man) will come with the glory of God. And in the Old Testament God appears always surrounded by angels. Jesus says that he also will come with angels, that is, sharing in the divinity.

MARIITA: "Jesus was poor and his message was for the poor. The rich and the proud may be ashamed of him and of his message, and in fact they *are* ashamed of him."

FELIPE: "People who are ashamed of humble clothes, of the *campesino*'s coarse cotton shirt, they're ashamed of Jesus and his message. And people who are proud of their fine cars, their elegant clothes, their luxurious houses, they're ashamed of Jesus too."

ARMANDO: "And he says that he will be ashamed of them, because false Christians are really a shame to him. He, who was a revolutionary, has disciples who are rich. He, who struggled so hard against the religious practices of the Pharisees, has seen his doctrine now converted into a purely religious rite, and his liberation into an opiate of the people. This must be a great shame for him."

I tell you truly
that there are some of those here present
who will not die
without having first seen
    the kingdom of God.

I said: "This is a very mysterious verse and I have never understood it clearly. A teacher of ours at the seminary who was a great biblical scholar couldn't give us a good explanation. But maybe you *campesinos* can discover the true interpretation."

MARIITA: "The kingdom of God isn't heaven, because he says some of them won't die without seeing it."

REBECA: "The kingdom of God is love, and people who love are beginning to see it."

OLIVIA: "But he says that *some* of those present there. He doesn't say 'all,' not even 'many.' Because most of them weren't going to believe in him and therefore weren't going to see that kingdom, which would be the kingdom of only a little group, the group of his followers united in love and having all things in common. The same thing can be said here in Solentiname. Many people don't come to these meetings and don't share in the kingdom of God which has already begun to exist in a little group. They haven't yet seen this kingdom and they don't know that it exists. That's the same thing that happened with the people who were listening to Jesus. Most of them didn't understand the kingdom of God even though it was right here in the middle of them."

FELIPE: "In this meeting we are having an experience of the kingdom."

ALEJANDRO: "Together with many in other little groups in Nicaragua and in many other parts of the world."

I said: "You have made me understand this verse quite clearly."

EPILOGUE

In October 1977, during a period of countrywide up-heaval, the Nicaraguan National Guard ravaged the Solentiname community. In December, writing from Costa Rica, Cardenal explained in a "Letter to the People of Nicaragua" why he had joined the Sandinista guerrillas. The following translation by William Barbieri is reprinted with permission of the National Catholic Reporter, Box 281, Kansas City, MO 64141.

Twelve years ago I arrived at Solentiname with two companions to found a small, contemplative community. Contemplation means union with God. We soon became aware that this union with God brought us before all else into union with the peasants, very poor and very abandoned, who lived dispersed along the shores of the archipelago.

Contemplation also brought us to the revolution. It had to be that way. If not, it would have been fake contemplation. My old novice master, Thomas Merton, the inspirer and spiritual director of our foundation, told me that in Latin America I could not separate myself from political strife.

In the beginning we would have preferred a revolution with nonviolent methods. But we soon began to

251

realize that at this time in Nicaragua a nonviolent struggle is not feasible. Even Gandhi would agree with us. The truth is that all authentic revolutionaries prefer nonviolence to violence; but they are not always free to choose.

The Gospel was what most radicalized us politically. Every Sunday in Mass we discussed the Gospel in a dialogue with the peasants. With admirable simplicity and profound theology, they began to understand the core of the Gospel message: the announcement of the kingdom of God, that is, the establishment on this earth of a just society, without exploiters or exploited, with all goods in common, just like the society in which the first Christians lived. But above all else the Gospel taught us that the word of God is not only to be heard, but also to be put into practice.

As the peasants of Solentiname got deeper and deeper into the Gospel, they could not help but feel united to their brother and sister peasants who were suffering persecution and terror, who were imprisoned, tortured, murdered; they were violated and their homes were burnt. They also felt solidarity with all who with compassion for their neighbor were offering their lives. For this solidarity to be real, they had to lay security, and life, on the line.

In Solentiname it was well known that we were not going to enjoy peace and tranquillity if we wanted to put into practice the word of God. We knew that the hour of sacrifice was going to arrive. This hour has now come. Now in our community everything is over.

There a school of primitive painting became famous throughout the world. Paintings, woodwork, and various handicrafts from Solentiname are sold not only in Managua, but also in New York, Washington, Paris, Venezuela, Puerto Rico, Switzerland, and Germany. Lately peasants from Solentiname had begun to write beautiful poetry. Their poems were published in Nicaragua and other countries.

Several films were made in Solentiname, one of them by BBC in London. Much has been written about Solentiname in various languages; records have been made, even in German. We have in that distant corner of the lake a great library gathered during a lifetime. We had a collection of pre-Columbian art found in Solentiname that grew through the years. We had a large guest house with plenty of beds for visitors. We had ovens for ceramics and a large shop for all kinds of handicrafts. There we worked with wood, leather, copper, bronze, and silver. We were also developing communal work for young peasants through a cooperative. The cooperative, with the help of a German institution, was about ready to begin a dairy and factory of European-style cheese.

It was said in Germany: "Solentiname is everywhere, it is the beginning of a more human world. It is a Christian life—not just waiting for a better world, but working for their neighbor's peace, for peace in nature, for peace within the community." In Venezuela it was said that "Solentiname is something so God-like and so much of this world that it is a place where poetry, painting, and the harvest do not divide people into poets and farmers, but constitute the solidarity of one life." Now all that is over.

Twelve years ago, when the apostolic nuncio approved my project to found a new monastery, he told me that he would have preferred that the community be established in a less remote place than Solentiname, because there we would have no visitors. The truth is that we were always flooded with visitors from Nicaragua and other countries. Many times they were people who arrived in Nicaragua only to visit Solentiname; sometimes they arrived directly by way of Los Chiles or San Carlos, without any interest in even visiting Managua. Abundant correspondence from all parts of the world arrived in Solentiname.

But now brush will grow once again where our community used to be, just as it did before our arrival. There, there was a peasant mass, there were paintings, statues, books, records, classes, smiles of beautiful children, poetry, song. Now all that is left is the savage beauty of nature. I lived a very happy life in that near paradise that was Solentiname. But I was always ready to sacrifice it all. And now we have.

One day it happened that a group of boys and girls from Solentiname, because of profound convictions and after having let it mature for a long time, decided to take up arms. Why did they do it? They did it for only one reason: for their love for the kingdom of God, for the ardent desire that a just society be implanted, a real and concrete kingdom of God here on earth. When the time came, these boys and girls fought with great valor, but they also fought as Christians. That morning at San Carlos, they tried several times with a loudspeaker to reason with the guards so they might not have to fire a single shot. But the guards responded to their reasoning with submachine gunfire. With great regret, they also were forced to shoot.

Alejandro Guevara, one of those from my community, entered the building when in it there were no longer any but dead or wounded soldiers. He was going to set fire to it so that there would be no doubt about the success of the assault, but out of consideration for the wounded, he did not do it. Because the building was not burned, it was officially denied that it was taken. I congratulate myself that these young Christians fought without hate—above all, without hate for the wounded guards, poor peasants like themselves, also exploited. It is horrible that there are dead and wounded. We wish that there were not a struggle in Nicaragua, but this does not depend upon the oppressed people that are only defending themselves.

Some day there will be no more war in Nicaragua, no more peasant guards killing other peasants. Instead there will be an abundance of schools, hospitals, and clinics for everyone, food adequate for everyone, art and entertainment. But most important, there will be love among all.

Now the repression that has gone on so long in the North has arrived at Solentiname. A tremendous number of peasants have had to flee, others are in exile, remembering those beautiful islands with their now destroyed homes. They would be there yet, living tranquil lives, dedicated to their daily tasks. But they thought of their neighbor, and of Nicaragua, and began to work for them.

I do not think about the reconstruction of our small community of Solentiname. I think of a task much more important that we all have—the reconstruction of the whole country.

On July 19, 1979, the Sandinista revolution was victorious. Many of the Solentiname community participated in the struggle against the Somoza dictatorship. Ernesto Cardenal is now Minister of Culture of Nicaragua.

Also from Orbis . . .

José Comblin
THE CHURCH AND
THE NATIONAL SECURITY STATE
"The best analysis thus far of the ideology, aims, and strategy of the national security state and the problems it poses for the Latin American church vis-à-vis existing authoritarian regimes. As the analysis shows, military governments in Latin America have cleverly adopted clerical language to pose as guardians of Christian values, principles, and traditions while progressively depriving their citizens of basic human rights. The church must respond to this situation, theologian Comblin believes, with a new pastoral strategy that actively defends human rights and effectively leads mankind to freedom and love. By clarifying the issues in the church-state confrontation, Comblin has made a major contribution to a fuller understanding of the Latin American context. North Americans particularly can profit from his thinking. Well-organized, closely reasoned but easily intelligible presentation. Informative appendix on the Peruvian military regime; notes; selected bibliography. Suitable for advanced undergraduate, graduate, and professional readers." *Choice*

"Packed with critical social, political and theological analysis, insight into Scripture and a sound conviction of what the gospel is all about. The book is most rewarding." *Missiology*
256pp. Paper $8.95

Julio de Santa Ana
TOWARDS A CHURCH OF THE POOR
"This volume is the third prepared by the World Council of Churches' Commission on the Churches' Participation in Development. In this volume there is a descriptive first section on 'The Churches and the Plight of the Poor,' and a second on 'The Challenge and Relevance of the Poor for the Church.' Both provide important materials for all of us in the affluent middle-class sector of the Church. It is to the third section however, and particularly the final chapter, that attention must be directed. There, ten proposals are listed touching on alignment, the Bible, theology, solidarity, involvement, struggle and conflict, education, formation of agents of change, assistance and justice, and structure."

> *Mennonite Publishing House Evaluation*

"Whereas the first two volumes were historical treatments of the relation of the Church to the poor, the present one is disturbingly contemporary. This book is not designed for experts, but for rank-and-file use across the board within the life of the Church. Readers in the latter constituency will find documentation, charts, and a stunning amount of bibliographical data collected in the footnotes (a tribute to the assiduous edition of Julio de Santa Ana) so that even the most skeptical will find a convincing case presented."

> *The Ecumenical Review*
> *236pp. Paper $8.95*

William J. O'Malley, S.J.
THE VOICE OF BLOOD:
Five Christian Martyrs of Our Time
"Anyone who has seen an issue of *Amnesty International*, with its documented cases of murder, torture and harassment by repressive regimes all over the world, will recognize the background for this agonizing and powerful account of modern-day martyrs. The author, a teacher, playwright and drama director, has taken the bare facts of the murders of five Jesuits in not dissimilar situations in El Salvador, Brazil and Africa during 1976-77 and written a story of suspense, exploitation, violence and Christian resistance that rivets the attention and commands a response."
Spiritual Book News

"Father O'Malley tells the stories of these men well, in simple but vivid terms. Together they spell out the demands that Christian discipleship continues to make in a world where the struggle for justice and freedom exacts a bitter price."
America

"O'Malley has embellished the lives of these men with an intense narrative on the social struggles which have demanded the involvement of the church to the point of sacrifice of life."
Library Journal
195pp. Paper $7.95